RTB: The Funny Side of My Aerospace Career

Dennis Hannaway

For privacy reasons, some names, locations, and dates may have been changed.

Book Cover designed by the author.

Chapter illustrations and chapter header illustrations by the author except:

"The Evil One," "A Tale of Two Petes,"
"At the Supermarket I & II," the crab for "Chinese Buffet,"
"I Just Wanted Time To Myself," and "Ski Trip"
by Polina Smirnova

"Dog Adoption I & II" by Judy King

Ms. Smirnova and Mrs. King graciously donated their art for this project.

First edition 2024

ISBN: 979-8-9913033-0-9

Thanks go out to my wife Laura for listening.

Infinite thanks go out to Lynn Azar for her friendship and her assistance editing.

The events described in this book are true. Names of certain individuals have been changed to protect the innocent...and the guilty.

Preface

RTB: Return To Base! You are about to read a collection of direct and indirect experiences along with events I have witnessed over the past 35 years. Why would it interest you? Because it's funny. It's the world seen through the eyes of an Aerospace Engineer; and not just an Aerospace Engineer, but a Flight Test Engineer that later became a Program Manager. So, imagine if you can, someone that spent four years training to be an objective analyst and allowed their imagination to wither away (the Engineer part), then developed a cynical, sardonic, edge to their personality with a dark sense of humor and an ability to notice things that most people can't (the Flight Test part) and finally assimilate to the "dark side" of the Aerospace program management. Think of the stories this person could tell!

Usually, these stories were told at times when mentoring was involved or when a life lesson was being discussed. Many times I was told, "You need to write this down."

This memoir contains stories that involve an aircraft flight test or two, and the coworkers at the aircraft companies. It doesn't contain discussions of test details or incidents – that's for another book a few years from now, perhaps *RTB 2*. There are tales of attempts at work-life balance from the overworked Flight Test Engineer perspective. Also, there are memories of college experiences. Why include college experiences in a memoir about an Aerospace career? I had a professor during my freshman year lecture us in class that our Aerospace career began in the college classroom. If we graduated, we would take the college experiences with us throughout our career and in all we do. He was correct.

Contents

HODAD

Did you ever have a co-worker that you could not help but dislike? I've had a few throughout my career, but none stands out like Simon.

Simon was a human carbon-copy of the used car salesman from the movie "True Lies" with his loud, arrogant, and bullying manner. He was a big talker. Always hyping himself and talking about how great he is. Simon claimed to have been a Formula One race car driver, played professional ball with the Cincinnati Reds, and caddied for Payne Stewart who then went on to sponsor him in the PGA for three years. He also claimed he was NFL player Lawrence Taylor's best man at Taylor's wedding. Probably the biggest lie Simon told was that he was an F-8 pilot.

Everyone in the office worked 10 hour days, except Simon. He had his own schedule. Simon shuffled into the office around 9:30AM. Simon dragged his feet when he walked. The bottoms of his boat shoes were probably worn down to the inner soles by his shuffle. He would slam his car keys and a newspaper onto his desk as he noisily rolled his chair out from under the desk and start his computer. He read the newspaper with his feet propped on his desk as the computer booted up. At 10:00AM, he would phone a friend located somewhere else at the facility and loudly talk about his greatness and demean his coworkers for the next 30 minutes. After an hour of surfing the internet, he'd leave to go home for lunch.

The afternoon routine was nearly identical. Simon would drag himself into the office at 2:30PM, slamming his keys on the desk. After looking at emails, he'd call an engineer at Honeywell to remind him that he needed a test plan for the Heads Up Display (HUD) *[He was plagiarizing the Honeywell plan into a test plan that was assigned to him]*. He then would call an FAA engineer at the Los Angeles Aircraft Certification Office to give him a completely bogus status report regarding the HUD test plan. After surfing the internet for a while, Simon ended the workday at 4:00PM. He also appeared in the office on Sundays to read the newspaper and watch sports on the internet. Simon regularly logged 48 hours work for the week.

Whenever he was assigned other work, there was always some excuse why he could not take on the new responsibility. On one occasion, Simon begrudgingly accepted the task to plan and conduct the tests for the Pilot compartment view in heavy rain. He wrongly provided status over the next several weeks that the plan was released, and all was ready for test execution. The test was scheduled for a weekend to take advantage of incoming weather. Simon claimed he couldn't work that weekend because he and his wife were flying to California for a wedding. Another flight test engineer was assigned at the last minute to conduct the test, only to discover that the test plan was never written.

One day, Simon's business card request came to our attention. The lead Avionics flight test engineer, Walt, and me were discussing upcoming test activities when Karl, the Chief Test Engineer, showed us the business card request. On the form, Simon gave himself the title:

HUD FLIGHT TEST PROJECT ENGINEER

I recommended showing the request to the actual HUD Project Engineer to get his approval, but Walt had a better idea.

Weeks later, Simon's business cards arrived. Simon eagerly tore open the box, but upon viewing the contents yelled, "Fuck this!" and threw the cards across the office and stormed out.

The business cards showed the company's name and Simon's name in accordance with the company's business card format, but his title showed only one word:

HODAD

Epilogue: The administrative assistant got a nice little card holder for Simon's cards and always had them on display on Simon's desk to which he would promptly swipe off his desk. Whenever one of the test airplanes would deploy for testing to places like Yuma, AZ or Roswell, NM, the flight test engineer would take a handful of Simon's business cards, distribute them among the travelers with instructions to leave them at bars and restaurants. Simon would receive phone calls and threats never to come to that establishment again.

Epilogue 2: About six months after receiving his business cards, Walt decided he wanted to take over the HUD project. That left Simon with nothing to do. Knowing his time was short, Simon quit the company.

Definition: HODAD – an obnoxious person that brags about themselves. A term typically used by surfers to describe non-surfers.

Confessional

I attended Parks College to study for a degree in Aerospace Engineering. The full name of the institution was Parks College of St. Louis University. Parks College was the Aviation and Engineering College of the University located in Cahokia, IL (the other colleges of the University were located on the Frost Campus in St. Louis). St. Louis University, or SLU (pronounced 'sloo' among the students), was a private university run by the Jesuits. The Parks campus was an old US Army Air Corps (USAAC) training facility built in the 1920s. Many of the buildings on the campus were from the original USAAC days. The Parks College offered Bachelor of Science degrees in Aerospace Engineering (AE), Avionics Engineering (AVE), Aircraft Maintenance Engineering (AME); Bachelor of Arts in Business Administration specializing in Professional Pilot Option (PPO) or in Transportation, Travel and Tourism (TTT or Triple T); and mechanic certification in Airframe and Powerplant (A&P).

The campus had two dormitories: Mercury Hall (aka, Merc) and Holloran Hall. Regardless of the dorm you were located in, freshman typically resided on the first floor, which was also called the "boom" floor. Upper classman resided in the upper floors; the top floor was designated as the "quiet" floor. Mercury Hall also had Father Lagesse's apartment on the second floor – Father Lagesse (aka, Padre) was the campus chaplain. I lived on first floor Merc during my freshman year.

As an AE student, exams always occurred on Fridays. For unknown reasons, the other degrees had exams on any day other than Friday; so, if you were an A&P, PPO or lower classman AME, your weekend started on Thursday night.

One particular Thursday night, my roommate and I were trying to study for the next day's exams. As usual, the A&Ps on the floor were raising hell. As the night continued passed midnight, we hoped the partying would become less noisy, but on this Thursday night, it seemed the partying was gaining momentum. Concentration was difficult, so it was time to ask the guys on the floor to quiet down a bit; and I had to take a bathroom break.

I stopped in the men's room down the hallway. It had eight toilet stalls, four urinals and eight sinks in the room. I entered a toilet stall, sat down, and proceeded to get on with my business. A few seconds later, I heard the sound of heaving and vomiting coming from the stall next to me. When I entered the men's room, I was so focused on how I would ask everyone to quiet down that I failed to notice a pair of feet slightly protruding from the stall door. Looking at the floor under the stall divider, I could see that someone was kneeling toward the toilet. An echoing voice emanating from the toilet bowl was gasping and crying, "Oh Lord, Oh Lord. Get me through this…"

Someone had too much to drink and was already face down in a toilet. Between gasps of "Oh Lord," the sick party-goer would vomit another toilet full of partially digested dinner. In between the sound of vomiting, I heard Dex, the A&P that was living in the dorm room next to me, entering the men's room asking if someone named Bill was in there. Dex noticed the legs and I heard him open the stall door next to mine, then say, "You're not Bill, sorry." And closed the door.

5

"Oh Lord. I'm going to die," the voice from the stall said again.

There are times when someone is completely defenseless and exposed. I couldn't resist. This was one of those times and I went for it.

"You have sinned, my son, and the Lord is exacting penance on you," I said, "what else will you confess?"

"What do you mean?" said the voice from the next stall.

"You are on your knees praying for the Lord's help. Surely, the sacrament of Confession is what you need for forgiveness."

Dex let out a loud laugh. I leaned forward, opened my stall door, exposing myself as I sat on the toilet with my shorts around my knees making "shut up" gestures with my hands. The guy kneeling over the toilet vomited again.

"What more do you have to confess, my son?" I asked.

"Uh…uh…I took ten dollars from my roommate…from his wallet…to buy beer tonight."

"Mmm. Thievery is a grave sin. What more is there?"

Cough. Cough. Spit.

Dex was biting his hand trying not to laugh too loud. I had successfully turned the toilet stall into a confessional.

"Padre? I cheated on my exam last week…*gasp*…I walked out of the bookstore without paying for a snickers bar…*cough…spit…cough…gasp…spit…*I…I…"

"I am here, my son," I said from behind the stall divider. Dex had shuffled out of the room. The drunk kid continued to vomit on occasion while praying in more ways than one for several minutes. I did my best to keep a straight steady voice and not laugh. Dex must have told others what was going on because I could hear other guys enter the men's room and giggle while the confession continued.

"Padre, I fucked my roommate's girlfriend when he was passed out last week...*cough...spit...*"

OK, game over I thought to myself. And my butt was getting sore from sitting on the toilet for too long.

"Now my son," I started, "Go back to your room and say ten 'Our Fathers' and ten 'Hail Marys' for penance. Come to the chapel this Sunday and we will pray together."

"Padre, I'm not Catholic," he said with an echo from the toilet bowl.

"We will work on that next," I replied.

Then I heard the sound of heavy breathing and a snore emanate from the stall. I knew my work was over. I got up and opened the door to my stall and there was Father Lagesse leaning against a sink looking right at me, along with five dorm mates standing around the men's room. For a moment I thought I was in deep shit. A huge amount of trouble.

"I expect to see you in the chapel, too" Padre said. The others in the room let out a round of applause and Padre smiled. "Leave the sacraments to me."

Fish Stick

A single man's pantry and refrigerator tells a lot about him. If the pantry has a little bit of everything and the refrigerator has more than just beer in it, then this man knows how to cook and prepares meals for himself. It doesn't have to be a well-stocked larder; but it is evidence of his culinary capabilities. A pantry containing a few cans of soup or a refrigerator that is 90% empty is evidence of a guy that eats out all the time. *Hint: The soup is for emergency use only.*

I fall into the "knows how to cook" category and my larder is usually well-stocked. As a single man, my pantry contained pasta, sauces, canned/jarred goods, spices, ingredients for recipes, etc. My refrigerator always had fruit, vegetables (bell peppers are candy to me), bacon, eggs, butter and beer; and my freezer usually contained at least a week's worth of meat. I always thought my palette was normal.

When I married, it was into an instant family with two step-children: one and a half and three years old. A larder that feeds children has some nasty stuff. It should not have surprised me. Less than 15 years earlier I was a kid and I remembered what was in my mother's pantry. But now married, this pantry contained kid-friendly things like Vienna sausages in a can (yuck!), breakfast cereal, and a million boxes of instant macaroni and cheese. The refrigerator and freezer were no better. Small

8

boxes of apple juice, frozen chicken potpies, French fries and fish sticks. Those 29 cent pot pies had no flavor. Frozen French fries just seemed wrong to me. Half the fries would be flat and burned when cooked to the recommended time and temperature. Frozen fish sticks were terrible: too dry and 80% batter.

It was one of those rare times when I was able to get off work at a "normal" time. Usually I was stuck in the office until 7PM, sometimes later, but not this day. My wife was going to collect the kids from the daycare, so I volunteered to prepare dinner. When I got home, I was starving. I searched the pantry for something to munch on while I prepped the kitchen for dinner. Nothing in the pantry. I checked the refrigerator but there was nothing for snacking. With hesitation, I checked the freezer. I didn't expect to find anything in there either, but what the hell, may as well try. There was nothing really in there but a bag of Gorton's fish sticks. I was not a fan of fish sticks (as previously explained). I took a fish stick out of the bag and bit half. It was cold and dry, but I was hungry, so I chewed and swallowed. Bearable, I thought. Screw it. I grabbed another stick, popped it in my mouth and put the bag back in the freezer.

A few minutes later I heard my wife's car entering the driveway. She unloaded the kids from their car seats, and everyone entered the kitchen from the side door. We kissed. She withdrew from the kiss and took a swing at me. I caught her arm in mid-swing.

"What the hell are you doing?" I asked with surprise.

"Who have you been with?!" she cried, "Your breath smells like pussy!"

Evil One

You know when your team respects you as their leader when they can say anything to you without fear of retaliation.

I had a team of 30 engineers and managers that reported directly and indirectly to me (I was a Director at the top of a matrix organization). Six of the team members had been coworkers of mine for ten years or longer – they knew me well. Ten of them were new to the company and the organization, ranging from a few months to less than two years. The remainder were somewhere in between.

I conducted a weekly program update meeting with the team. Supplier milestones was one of the topics in the meeting. The team had twelve suppliers that were developing various components of a flight control system for an airplane. Most of the suppliers were maintaining the mandatory 85% or better on-time performance of their deliverables; however, two suppliers were below performance. One was consistently around 70%-75% on-time for this quarter. The other was consistently terrible: less than 20% on-time performance. Ten engineers worked with the bad supplier, including one of the most senior engineers named Mort. He and I had worked on several programs over the past 10 years. Several milestones for this particular supplier were co-owned by Mort.

For each milestone that was missed, Mort stated that he could not proceed because the supplier was not providing the input he requested. After hearing the same response over and over again, I told Mort that he needed to either go to the supplier's facility and provide guidance or complete the work on his own.

Mort didn't like my suggestion. He glared at me and in a serious deadpan manner he said, "You are truly the Evil One."

The younger engineers in the room were quiet with their eyes wide open in disbelief. A few of the senior engineers quietly chuckled or smirked, shaking their heads. I knew Mort was frustrated and he meant no disrespect. It was his way of saying that he was not happy with the situation the supplier put on him and that he also knew he had to do as I directed.

I replied, "Thank you for bypassing 'mid-evil' and going straight to evil."

That earned smiles from all around the room.

My office was located on the side of the building that did not receive direct sunlight. There was a ventilation duct in the ceiling in the center of my office. It blew cold air no matter what time of the year, so the room was always ten degrees below desired temperature.

Later that day, I walked into my office to see this sign:

It's cold in here because his

𝕰𝖛𝖎𝖑

𝕻𝖗𝖊𝖘𝖊𝖓𝖈𝖊

sucks the warmth from you!

The arrow pointed at my chair. I loved it. I took it as a sign of respect. It gave my office a great atmosphere because as soon as you walked in and faced my desk, you saw a framed certificate for my Tae Kwon Do Third Degree Black Belt over my right shoulder and the Evil One sign over my left.

Human Resources didn't like it. The HR representative that frequently barged into my office (without invitation) demanded to know who made the sign and that I take it down. I told her I took no offense and that she should focus her concerns elsewhere.

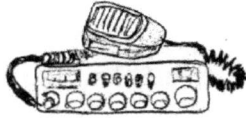

Asleep at the Wheel

There was a period of time in my life when I lived in southern California that my home was in Lancaster, and I worked in Long Beach. It was exactly 100 miles from my driveway to the parking lot at the Douglas Aircraft Company. Los Angeles area traffic was challenging at any time of day or night, including the outlying areas such as Simi Valley, Pomona, El Centro and my area, the Antelope Valley. Like many commuters from the Antelope Valley, my truck was equipped with a CB radio. The CB radio was important for receiving traffic reports of obstacles, signal alerts and general road conditions while a driver was still miles away from the problem and able to find an alternate route. The radio was also used for idle chat to occupy one's time while stuck in traffic. This was before cell phones were available – CBs were much safer to use while driving. The Antelope Valley CB radio community was a close knit group. My CB handle was "Aerolord." It was based on a radio call sign I had from my job. Through my CB radio, I became friends with 100 fellow commuters.

Morning rush hour in the LA basin started around 6:00AM. To avoid as much of it as possible, I usually began my commute from Lancaster to Long Beach around 4:30AM. Leaving that early allowed me to get to my desk around 6:45 – 7:00AM. This meant I was out of bed by 3:30AM, giving me almost an hour for my morning routine including a shower and coffee so I'd be alert for the drive. From my house, I would get on the Antelope Valley Freeway (CA-14) to head south toward LA.

As soon as a driver with a CB would get on the highway, one was to greet the commuter traffic with "Good morning Channel 12!" then identify yourself. Within seconds, every driver with a CB within range of your signal would wish you a good morning. The CA-14 portion of the commute from Lancaster to Interstate 5 (I-5) was 45 miles. If a CB commuter made good time, he or she would stop at the Carl's Jr restaurant off the Newall Ave exit for a restroom break and coffee refill before entering the LA valley. The Carl's Jr stop also allowed me the chance to meet a CB friend face-to-face for a few minutes. Interesting how we talked regularly every day, but almost never met.

On one particular Monday, it was a struggle for me to engage in my usual morning regime. I got coffee started, then took a shower. Drank coffee, got dressed. Then had more coffee as I switched between watching the Weather Channel, ABC World News Now and a cable movie channel. At the usual time, I got in my truck, then backed out of my driveway…

…then I was shaken awake by a stranger saying, "Hey dude, you need to wake up." That's all I remember. What follows is what I was told.

My truck was seen merging onto southbound CA-14 toward LA. "Inspector" recognized my red truck with its five foot roof mounted antenna, and greeted me on the CB, "Morning Aerolord, Inspector."

No response.

"Aerolord, this is Inspector. Good morning."

No response. Inspector assumed I may have been talking privately on another channel, so he stopped hailing me and greeted someone else.

Other morning CB commuters spotted my truck as I drove along the highway.

"Aerolord, good morning. Wildman..."

"Aerolord, good morning. Boyscout..."

"Good morning Aerolord, Librarian..."

"Legal Beagle" finally got a response from me. She said I responding to her salutation with gibberish. She thought I was being funny. Beagle tried to get me to talk about my weekend, but I wasn't making sense. "Snow Goose" was in the lane next to me, about a car length behind. He caught up to my broadside and looked into the cabin. He used a flashlight to try to get my attention, but I was unresponsive. Snow Goose concluded I was semi-conscious at the wheel. I was on "autopilot" and was reacting well to the traffic conditions, but I was asleep enough to be unaware consciously of what I was doing.

Two additional CB commuters drove near to my truck to keep other traffic away from me. I was near the halfway point along the CA-14 route when I was discovered to be asleep at the wheel. News of my condition was relayed throughout the CB community. One CBer was a retiree that went by the handle "Canyon Country." He had a base station that broadcasted at over 100 watts and he was awake in the early hours to talk to the commuters. Canyon Country and others constantly broadcasted to me to meet them at Carl's Jr for coffee. My responses were gibberish, but according to Boyscout, he saw me exit the highway at the Newall Ave off-ramp. "Straw Hat" saw me enter the parking lot of Carl's Jr, parking in an empty space near the other commuters. My truck stayed parked with the engine running for a few minutes. They hoped I would be awake, but I didn't exit the vehicle. Straw Hat approached my truck to see me with my head tilted back against the headrest of the seat with my mouth wide open. He opened the driver door, put my truck in Park, lowered the window and turned off the truck. Straw Hat recommended to the growing group of CB friends in the parking lot that someone should wake me in an hour and explain to me what had happened. "Pole Cat" shook me awake an hour later.

It is amazing what your mind and body will do when specific routines become deeply ingrained. Many of the CB commuters had been performing the 100+ mile daily round trip for years. If you do it so often, you could be spending at least one-third of your waking hours driving. The CB was a great distraction to the grueling traffic. On this occasion, it likely saved my life.

What's in a Name?

I coached kid's sports. My step-children were active in baseball and soccer; and I coached their teams. My step-daughter, Sarah, started playing soccer when she was five years old. The first year we lived in Savannah, Sarah was on a team whose coach focused only on the development of his daughter. His name was Mahmoud. His daughter played every position and the entire match. There were two or three girls that never played. I am not a "PC" parent, but I believe that unless a child is a savant at something, it will be around the age of nine or ten that they will "get it" after three years of practice. I was not happy with this Mahmoud as a coach. He would not allow other parents to assist. He was also vocal about his non-American upbringing, thus being a superior football player and the only person able to properly teach the sport.

The next soccer season, we found Sarah a new team. The new coach, Sam, played in the local adult league. He was proactive in having two assistant coaches and a team mom involved in an under eight year old (U8) girls team. Sam was a skills and technique style coach. Swarm ball was for five year olds: this team was going to learn to communicate and work together.

Amazingly, the girls made large strides playing as a team after the first few practices. The team mom did a great job coordinating among the parents and helped the girls to get to know each other. A pack of eight year old girls can go from a serious soccer team to a bunch of screaming idiots in no time. When debating a name for the team, the girls were tossing around suggestions like "the kittens," "puff girls" and "muffins".

"You girls are nothing but trouble," one of the mom's said. There it was. The perfect name for a bunch of eight year old girls: The Trouble.

The Trouble stayed together as a team for five years, until high school pulled them apart. During their time together, they were the most formidable team in their age group. Only one other team gave them competition. That team was coached by one of the local attorneys. Their team also stayed together for many years. The team had a set of twins whose name was M'Stardt, but the girls called them the Mustard twins. The twins were fast as lightning with their seemingly psychic connection. They were also notorious for double teaming an opponent. One time they high-lowed Sarah, severely knocking the wind out of her, resulting in both benches clearing for an insane punching, kicking, hair-pulling brawl that required all coaches and referees to break it up.

On one of the other teams was a girl with average soccer skills but a lot of passion for the game. She would be a really good player in the future because we coaches noted how she was learning from our team. This girl had an unfortunate name. Latreen. Her full name was Latreen Banyo. I had to check the spelling when I learned of her name. Her parents must have been oblivious of the French and Spanish languages. Thankfully Latreen's name wasn't spelled as its correct equivalent would be in those languages.

One match between the two teams was difficult for me and a few of the multilingual spectators to handle when Latreen's mother yelled, "Latreen! Latreen! Latreen Banyo! Get the shit out of your ass and get that ball!"

I swear you can't make this up.

A Tale of Two Petes

I studied Aerospace Engineering at Parks College in Cahokia, IL. The full name of the institution was Parks College of St. Louis University. Parks College was the Aviation and Engineering College of the University located in Cahokia, IL (the other colleges of the University were located on the Frost Campus in St. Louis). The Parks campus was an old US Army Air Corps training facility built in the 1920s. The student body averaged 800 students in the 1980s of which approximately 400 lived on campus in the two dormitories, Mercury Hall and Holloran Hall.

There are some interesting characters that attend small, private colleges. One such character was "Parachute Pete". He was an Airframe and Powerplant (A&P) student. Despite his small stature, he was destructive and crazy with a "don't give a shit" attitude. He got his nickname "Parachute" because he made a parachute out of bedsheets and jumped off buildings with it.

Parachute Pete's dormitory roommate was Pat, who to this day is one of my close friends. Pat had the unfortunate discovery of

Parachute's strangeness before everyone else. Pat entered their dorm room at the end of a long day of classes to find Parachute masturbating to a life sized magazine spread of a bikini model taped to his closet door. Needless to say, Pat was reassigned to a different dorm room.

One weekend as I was walking across campus, I noticed another friend, Oscar, standing near the northeast corner of Mercury Hall. He was shielding his eyes with his hand against the glare reflected from the windows as he looked up toward the top of the building.

"Hey Oscar, what are you looking for?" I asked.

"We should see something spectacular in a few moments," he replied.

The sound of an approaching scream was heard from the top of Mercury Hall, followed with a shout of "TERMINAL VELOCITY" as Parachute Pete ran across the roof of the building. He leapt up into the air when he ran out of roof, then plummeted straight down two stories with his homemade parachute fluttering behind him. He impacted a cantilevered awning above the side entrance to the dorm, then flipped over and fell another eight feet to the ground.

We were dumbfounded by the display. After a momentary delay, Oscar and I ran over to Pete asking if he was all right. Pete claimed he was OK and got to his feet with a little help from us. It was amazing that he did not have a severe injury.

"What do you think went wrong?" Oscar asked Parachute Pete.

"Not enough altitude for the chute to reef," Pete speculated.

A few months later, Parachute Pete tried another jump with his homemade bedsheet parachute off the top of the 17 story Greisedieck Hall at the St. Louis University main campus. According to eyewitness reports, he ran off the roof and had similar results to his previous jump off of Mercury Hall.

His chute fluttered behind him as he fell three floors,

then he impacted a canvas awning, which he ripped allowing him to fall through,

then took out a window air conditioning unit as he dropped another story

and fell onto another canvas awning. A third awning prevented him from falling any further. The campus security had to call the city fire department to send a ladder truck to get him down. Once again, Pete survived with only sprains to his wrist and ankle.

If one crazy guy named Pete wasn't enough, there was another attending the school at the same time: Psycho Pete.

Psycho Pete had been a Marine. It was never discovered what the status of his discharge was. We assumed it was honorable because he claimed he was on the GI bill. Psycho Pete was an average sized man, good looking with short wavy hair. But at times he would get a wild wide-staring look in his eyes and tilt his head to one side. Then the facial twitches would start. The episodes would last a few minutes. If you asked him if he was ok, he would explode that there was nothing wrong with him. Some students nicknamed him "Shell-shocked" but as his behavior became more widely known, the moniker "Psycho Pete" took hold.

Parks College had a radio station on the campus in Airport Hall, WPKS 101.5-FM. Airport Hall was a one story building with four classrooms in the northern half. Administrative offices and the radio station were in the southern half. I was doing my evening Dee Jay slot one weeknight, cueing a record when I heard a knock on the window. I opened the window to see Psycho Pete in military fatigues plus helmet with his face covered in camouflage paint and cradling what looked like an M16 semi-automatic rifle. He was laying on the ground between the side of the building and some bushes.

"Hey Pete, how are you doing?" I asked.

"How'd you know it's me?" Pete replied.

"Lucky guess," I said. "What are you doing?

"I'm tracking the security guard."

"Why"

"Do you think those pussies can protect us if the perimeter is penetrated?"

"Who's going to penetrate the perimeter, Pete?"

"The god damned locals, that's who!"

"Oh, good point. Hey Pete, hold on. I need to do a station ID… 'You're listening to WPKS, 101.5 FM. That was 'Cocaine' by Eric Clapton. Next up is something more appropriate given what I've just seen. 'Bad Moon Risin' by CCR.'"

"Hey Pete," I said turning back toward him, "Lloyd's pretty old. He's probably going to retire in a few months. Don't give him a heart attack." Lloyd was the nighttime campus security guard.

"Nah, nothing like that," Pete replied. "I'm just helping out on patrol. I'm going. If you see something weird, send a signal. Pull a fire alarm or something."

"Yeah, ok Pete. Keep your head down," I said. He crawled off behind the bushes, blending into the night.

Parks was too small a campus for two insane personalities to occupy at the same time. Whether Parachute and Psycho would be friends or enemies would be a losing scenario for the rest of the students living on-campus. Eventually the two did meet and became friends. For a few weeks, the two Petes created all sorts of mischief. Sometimes at night there would be the sound of gunfire emanating from the bean field next to the campus – gunfire or fireworks. Parachute also accompanied Psycho on evening "patrols" terrorizing students with bottle rockets and laying smoke to hide their escape.

The "Pete" honeymoon didn't last long. Parachute Pete had a younger sister that came to visit on a weekend when a fraternity sponsored a party in the student lounge. Parachute introduced his sister to Psycho Pete since Psycho was his best friend. After a night of loud music and lots of beer, Psycho Pete and Parachute's sister hooked up. Parachute Pete was furious and the hunt was on.

A few days later, Parachute Pete finally caught up to Psycho Pete. Psycho was in one of the shower rooms on the second floor of Mercury Hall. Parachute Pete repelled from the third floor men's room down to the second floor men's room adjacent to the shower room. He stripped naked and rigged the men's room door closed with a broom stick and his discarded clothes. Parachute Pete then brandished a knife and attacked Psycho Pete in the shower.

A student tried to enter the men's room but was unable to open the door because it was jammed. He got help from a few other students and they forced the door open. A curious student entered the shower room and found two naked Petes lying on the wet shower floor unconscious. The knife was near the door. It was concluded that they slipped on the wet, soapy floor as they wrestled for the knife, and impacted their heads when they fell, knocking themselves out.

It goes without mentioning…they were expelled.

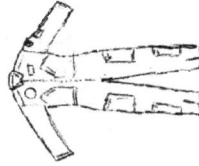

The Big Green Bird

There was a restaurant-lounge near the Savannah International Airport called "Bailey's Cockpit." It was a circular structure in the middle of a retention pond in front of the Days Inn Airport motel. The owner/manager was a gentleman named Robyn, who was also the first friend I made when I moved to Savannah.

The lounge was secured to pilings above the pond which was six to seven feet at its deepest point, but that didn't prevent the building from shaking when it was near full capacity. Three-quarters of the circular building was the lounge area with panoramic windows allowing a view of the pond, motel and airport. The kitchen was in the remaining one-quarter of the building. A square-shaped bar was in the center of the lounge.

The Cockpit was a popular place. It was always filled to near capacity during lunch hours. Robyn had the full staff on duty during lunch: two cooks, two bartenders and four waitresses. The cockpit staff was all female except for one cook. Happy Hour started around 3PM with the lounge filled beyond capacity, going well into the early evening. Robyn was at the Cockpit during the lunch shifts, sometimes staying through happy hour.

The Cockpit staff was an interesting and occasionally dysfunctional group. Robyn's wife, Shelley, worked there as the manager and bussed tables during busy times. Lisa was the assistant manager; she waitressed during lunch and tended bar during happy hour. Kim and Kathy were tall, busty waitresses that unintentionally provided most of the entertainment in the lounge by just watching them cope with serving food and drinks. Sarah and Shannon were friends since elementary school and roommates. And there was Tommy the cook, a tall, thin black man that looked to be 16 years old.

The Savannah International Airport was the old Travis Air National Guard Field. The 165th ANG Air Wing was stationed at the airport. The Beaufort Marine Air Base was 50 miles to the northeast. The Jacksonville Naval Air Station was 100 miles to the south. The Savannah airfield was a convenient base of operations for visiting squadrons from the Air Nation Guard, US Air Force or NATO to use for training purposes with the neighboring Marine and Naval bases. The visiting military pilots and support crews stayed at the Days Inn and frequented the Cockpit. On a Thursday or Friday afternoon, if you heard the sounds of afterburners near the airport, it could be concluded that the Cockpit would have a busy happy hour.

One week in the mid-1990s, the airport was filled with the sounds of F-15 and Eurofighter engines. A US Air Force and a United Kingdom Royal Air Force fighter squadron were using the airport as fixed base operations while conducting training exercises in the airspace just off the coast. Robyn and his staff were pleased because it meant his lounge would see a lot of business from the visiting air crews.

I stopped at the Cockpit for Friday Happy Hour. The lounge had been full of green flight suits for over an hour before I got there. Every seat was full and the walkaway surrounding the circular lounge had patrons drinking beer and leaning over the railings looking at the fish in the pond. A British pilot sitting at the bar had been trying to coerce Lisa into giving him a round of drinks on the house, while also using his best

Brit charms to "chat her up." Lisa was the one Cockpit employee that did not give away alcohol. The other bartenders or waitresses would provide a free round on occasion to a regular patron or someone that spent a lot of money, but Lisa never did. Lisa also had a boyfriend that was a manager for final assembly at the aircraft manufacturer located at the airport. She had her standards and they were pretty high.

"Come on, Lisa," I heard the Brit pilot say, "a round of bevvie would keep me and the chaps here a while longer."

"I don't do that," Lisa replied. "Ask Mr. Dennis, I've never bought a man a drink in my bar."

"That's true," I said nodding toward Lisa, "not me, nor her boyfriend."

Tommy strolled out of the kitchen to pour himself a soda from the waitress station. He had been asking for refreshment for a while, but the waitresses were running at full speed serving the customers.

"I been in dat kitchen all day," Tommy said to me. "They sho is eatin' and drinkin'."

The British pilot kept begging Lisa for a round of beer and suggesting they get to know each other better. His fellow fliers were teasing him about his lack of success. I knew Lisa very well and usually she would be very annoyed by now, but she was handling the situation well, or I had thought so until I heard her say, "If you jump naked in the pond from the roof, I'll buy you a round."

That comment drew jeers from the other pilots. The potential suitor laughed it off. Tommy began telling me about a car wash business he wanted to do on the side. He was always looking for ways to make more money. As Tommy talked, I noticed the people on the walkway outside were all looking upward. Then, an empty green flight suit glided into the pond.

"I jus' saw a big green bird," Tommy said alarmingly.

A naked body flew off the roof and into the pond. Half the people on the walkway were wet from the splash. All the British aircrew roared in laughter. The naked pilot swam to his flight suit, performed a few water ballet tricks, and then crawled out of the pond. He wrapped his wet flight suit around his waist and between his legs, looking as if he was wearing a big wet green diaper. He re-entered the lounge and Lisa dutifully poured him a draft beer.

As does one, as will others do…especially if alcohol is involved. Within minutes, flight suits and naked bodies were plunging into the pond off the roof of the lounge. The drunken diving didn't last long because one of the visitors got injured by a bent shingle nail on the roof. Robyn summed it up best, "It's all fun and games until someone tears their scrotum."

At the Supermarket I

Grocery store weirdness can be as interesting as the Walmartian pictures you see on the internet. I witnessed several hilarious events at grocery stores. One in particular occurred at a Kroger parking lot in the Savannah area.

While searching for a place to park my truck, I had to yield for a Kroger employee riding one of the electric scooter shopping carts through the parking lot. This was one of the electric scooters meant for disabled persons to use instead of a wheelchair. Unfortunately, the scooters are left haphazardly in the lot after the last user drives off in their vehicle and employees go fetch them to return them to the store entrance. The scooter battery became depleted about 50 feet from the entrance. The employee riding the scooter attempted to push the scooter into the store entrance but had no success moving it. She abandoned the scooter to get help from coworkers from inside the store.

Meanwhile, a car pulled into a disabled parking spot along the side of the store. A woman, likely in her 70's and obese, struggled out of her car; pulled a folding walker out of the backseat and started maneuvering her way between her car and the car parked beside her. Also, four rows away from the entrance, another old and obese woman struggled out of her vehicle brandishing a cane. Both women locked their sights on the abandoned scooter simultaneously. The Walker Woman tossed her walker aside and bolted for the scooter. At the same time, the Cane Lady dropped her cane and ran.

I participated in Track and Field in High School. I wasn't the fastest athlete on the team, but I could run a 40 yard dash with the best of them. I saw the two old and obese women run faster than anything I could have done when I was seventeen. Both women made it to the scooter simultaneously and proceeded to slap, punch, scratch, spit, pull hair and curse in the most pathetic, yet incredibly funny catfight I had ever seen. After a minute of melee, Walker Woman was able to push Cane Lady away causing Cane Lady to fall backwards. Walker Woman mounted the scooter and attempted to get away. The scooter moved a few tiny inches and promptly died again. She tried rocking the scooter forward and backward from the seat but to no avail. Cane Lady got up and pushed Walker Woman off the scooter. Cane Lady jumped on and also failed to move the scooter. Cane Lady was wrestled off the scooter and the combat continued. A den of brave Girl Scouts that were selling cookies at the store entrance ran over to the elderly combatants hoping to break up the catfight. As the young girls tried to separate the human equivalent of parking lot water buffaloes, a teenage store employee walked over to the shopping scooter with a small vehicle battery, clamped the electrode leads onto the dead battery terminals, straddled the scooter saddle and drove the scooter into the store.

Twenty minutes later as I was leaving the store, I saw an ambulance in the parking lot with lights flashing. Paramedics were administering oxygen to the old women. It also looked like the Girl Scouts sold half their cookie supply to the paramedics.

Pizza Call

I lived in Lancaster, CA for a while in the 1990s. Back then, it was a desert city of approximately 100,000 residents. Palmdale, to the immediate south, had about 70,000 people. Both cities had significant numbers of aerospace families. The Aerospace and Defense industry was big in the area with Edwards AFB, Lockheed Skunk Works, McDonnell Douglas Phantom Works, Northrop B-2 production, Jet Propulsion Laboratory and NASA Dryden all within the vicinity. And yet there also resided many non-aerospace families, and I suspect what I am about to describe involved a non-aerospace family.

It was a recurring event every Friday night around 7:30PM. The phone would ring. Either my wife or I would answer, "Hello?"

"Hi, I'd like to order a large pizza for delivery," the voice on the phone would say.

"Uh, you have the wrong number," I'd reply.

When it first started, the call happened only once on Friday night. As the weeks went by, it grew to two, maybe three calls in one night.

Rinnngg!

"Hello?"

"Hi, I'd like to order a large pizza for delivery."

"You have a wrong number."

Three minutes later…*Rinnngg!*

"Hello?"

"Hi, I'd like to order a large pizza for delivery."

"You have a wrong number, again."

"Isn't this Major Tom's Pizza?"

"No, it's not. Look it up again."

Three months into the ordeal, it was getting nasty.

Rinnngg!

"Hello?"

"Hi, I'd like to order a large pizza for delivery."

"You have a wrong number."

"Don't fuck with me. I know this is Major Tom's Pizza!"

"Nope. Why don't you order from someplace else?"

"Fuck you. I want to order a pizza."

This guy could not break the cycle of habitually calling the wrong number and he would not take the suggestion to order from somewhere else. Fighting back in a passive/aggressive manner wasn't working. Blocking his phone number would involve the phone company. Then the solution dawned on me.

Rinnngg!

"Hello?"

"Hi, I'd like to order a large pizza for delivery."

"Ok. What would you like?"

"A large Hawaiian pizza with garlic bread."

"Ok, your usual order."

"Yeah, that's right."

"Ok. Should be there in 20 minutes."

"Great, thanks. Bye."

About 40 minutes later…*Rinnngg!*

"Hello?"

"Hey. I ordered a large Hawaiian 40 minutes ago. It ain't here."

"Oh yeah, the driver should be there any minute now. He had a few stops where the customer was looking for cash. I was about to call you..."

"Huh? Ok. A few minutes you say?"

"Yep. When the driver called, he said he was heading your way."

"Ok. I'll wait for him."

"Thanks, bye."

Fifteen minutes later…*Rinnngg!*

"Hello?"

"Where the fuck is my pizza?!"

"What pizza?

"Don't gimme that shit! I ordered a pizza that should have been here an hour ago! Where the fuck is it?!"

"I don't like your attitude. You're not getting a pizza." And I hung up. There were no more phone calls that night.

The following Sunday morning, I noticed an article in the newspaper about an arrest made at a Major Tom's Pizza in Palmdale. A man arrived at the restaurant and got into an altercation with the store manager about a pizza delivery that never happened. The store manager and the man got into a fight. Police were called to break it up. The manager was badly bruised but refused medical attention. The man that started the fight was arrested. After reading the news article, I suspected I knew why that fight started. I looked up the Major Tom's location in the phone book.

I quickly discovered why I was receiving the phone calls for a pizza order. Lancaster and Palmdale were in the same area code. Lancaster utilized a 988 phone number prefix. Palmdale had a 987 prefix. The Major Tom's in Palmdale and my home phone number had the same last four digits.

Best Dog

My final year at Douglas Aircraft Company was one of the best I had when I worked there. I was a member of the Flight Test Engineering Stability and Control team. There were five on the team: me, Marcus, Liam, Mallie and John. Malena, or 'Mallie' for short, had been an employee since 1989 and a good S&C engineer. John, Marcus, Liam and I worked together on previous Flight Test programs such as the C-17 and MD-87. We were a great team and enjoyed working together.

Liam, Marcus and I would go to lunch each day. The weekly lunch plan was Liam's duty by choice. Each day had a specific location. Monday was 'Mighty Grinder' on the other side of the airport. Tuesday was 'Best Thai' in Lakewood. Wednesday was 'Uncle Bill's Tavern.' Thursday was 'Johnny Reb's Southern Barbeque.' Friday was the 'Germania Deli'.

It was Tuesday. Lunch time approached and Liam asked in his Scottish-Jamaican lilt, "Boys, Best Dog?"

The Best Thai restaurant was called "Best Dog" by most patrons, a tasteless joke that would likely draw a disciplinary action from Human Resources in today's politically correct world. The three of us piled into Marcus' Cadillac for the drive. Best Dog was located in a strip mall on the corner of Bellflower and Del Amo Boulevards in Lakewood, just a few blocks from our office. The strip mall also included a locksmith, a laundromat, a doughnut shop and a country western bar.

The restaurant had six small tables that would tightly sit four people each. The entrance to the kitchen was a maze-like partition with numerous cast iron skillets hanging on the wall facing the dining area. The menu had only two items: curry chicken or curry beef. Both entrees were served on a half cup of steamed white rice. It also came with a salad that consisted of a slice of cucumber, a single sliced ring of raw onion and a black olive drizzled in corn syrup. The only beverage offered was tap water, no ice. The curry was ok. The meal cost $1.95 – you couldn't beat the price.

Liam had been going to Best Dog for the past five years. When we walked in, a Thai lady presumably the owner in her late 40s/early 50s and only 4'9" tall shuffled over to greet Liam and guided us to our usual table. As was her routine, she handed out menus despite us already knowing there were only two items listed.

"Curry beef, Mr. Liam? Extra rice?" she asked as she placed our water in front of us.

"Yes, please," replied Liam.

"Curry beef for you sirs?"

"Yep." "Yes, thanks," we replied.

In less than a minute, the lady returned with the small plates containing the "salad." A few minutes later, she returned with the curries and rice.

"I have new cook," the lady said, "good food now better. You tell me you like." Promptly she turned and walked away.

There was more gravy in the curry than usual, but it looked and tasted like the same dish we had many times in the past. We had the typical conversation about work while we ate. Marcus mentioned that his foot pain was getting worse. He had been limping for a few days now.

We finished our meal. The lady approached the table and asked, "How was curry, Mr. Liam?"

"It was ok. It was soupy, but ok," Liam said leaning on his elbow and gesturing with his hand.

"No. Oh no, no. No soap in food," the lady said aghast.

"Not soapy," Liam tried to explain. "Soupy. Like soup."

"Oh. Oh, soap in food," the lady said shaking her head in twittering fashion, "I fix!"

With that, she marched toward the kitchen, snatching the largest cast iron skillet off the wall as she passed. Suddenly a high pitched female voice was emanating from the kitchen speaking in (presumably) Siamese. A vocal exchange ensued as a male voice spoke up speaking the same language. The vocal banter went back and forth, getting louder. We looked at each other, eyes wide open.

"Holy shit Liam," I said, "you started a fight."

"The fuck I did," Liam replied.

"She thinks there is soap in the food," Marcus observed as he reached for his wallet.

The two voices from the kitchen were yelling at each other simultaneously.

KABONG!!!!!! The sound of metal striking bone. A small man came staggering out of the kitchen with both hands against his bloodied head. He made his way to the restaurant exit as the lady ran out of the kitchen. She leapt into the air and grasping the skillet handle with two hands wound her arms around as if hammering a stake and brought the skillet down on the man's head with such force he flew out the exit into the parking lot.

"NO SOAP IN FOOD!!" the lady yelled and threw the skillet at the man lying on the ground. She stormed back in the kitchen yelling something and sounds of metal objects being thrown followed.

Our heads snapped around with eyes and mouths wide open.

"Fuck that! Let's get the fuck out of here!" Liam said. We bolted out of chairs and ran to the car. Marcus paused for a second to look at the injured man, but the lady was running toward him with another skillet in her hand.

"Marcus! Car! Now!" Liam yelled. Marcus ran to the Caddy. We jumped in. Marcus tore out the parking lot, heading back to the office in the midday traffic. Marcus asked what we should do. Liam said something about calling the police when we got to the facility, which he did anonymously from the parking lot guard booth. A police dispatcher mentioned they were already alerted to the situation.

Best Dog was taken off the list of lunch stops. About three weeks later, we were heading out to lunch on a Tuesday. Liam suggested we drive by Best Dog. It was closed with yellow CAUTION tape across the entrance in a big X. Looking through the windows, we saw chairs turn upside down on tabletops; otherwise, it looked as it did the last time we were there.

We went to the country western bar across the parking lot. As the waitress handed us menus, Liam asked, "What's with the Thai place over there?"

"The owner attacked one of her employees," the waitress replied, "Really messed up the guy."

Marcus' eyes got wide. Liam's mouth fell open. I kept a straight face asking, "What happened to the owner?"

"Don't know. She was taken away by the police. The guy left by ambulance. The place closed that day. So do you guys know what you want?"

"What's the soup of the day?" asked Liam.

Marcus and I threw our menus at him.

Shit Baby

I worked for a major aerospace company in Southern California in the 1980s. About a year into this job, my department hired a college graduate name Rick. He was a skinny kid from the Midwest who had a slight build and probably weighed no more than 120 pounds. He also had long, thin curly hair along with what could be described as a "cheesy" mustache. Rick was a good guy, always eager to learn new things.

Rick was also a practical joker. You never wanted Rick to discover your home address or phone number. He would take the subscription cards out of magazines and fill out a free three-month trial subscription with an unsuspecting person's address. He never used their names, instead he would use the names of professional wrestlers. Coworkers would receive magazines for "M. A. Choman" or "Hogan Hulkster: or "Mr. Fuji." He would also choose the most inappropriate magazine for a particular person. Neal, a single man that just started a new relationship, received *Baby Today*, a magazine about newborn care. Larry received a periodical about gay relationships and dating – it didn't go over well with his wife. Rick crossed the line when Roddie received *High Times*, inappropriate for an aerospace engineer. Not to mention the harassing mails and phone calls they would receive for unpaid subscriptions.

Rick never seemed to eat. If he joined us for lunch, he would not order anything. He claimed he almost never went grocery shopping because he would go to happy hours and eat off the free food trays.

A few months after Rick started in the office, he returned from the New Year's break with the announcement that he was married. He did "the deed" with his college girlfriend. He had not mentioned her before, so it was strangely surprising that he came back married. It was a Vegas wedding. He showed us pictures of himself and his new wife on their wedding night: Rick dressed in an oversized zebra striped suit (yes, a zebra striped suit) and his wife donned a skintight multicolored vinyl catsuit, like a dominatrix. Rick's wife was the opposite of him. She was very large, over 300 pounds. Her limbs were very large too. I doubt that she could stand with her ankles together or bend over to touch her knees. The photo gave the appearance that they were an odd couple: short, thin Rick and tall obese spouse. But he loved her, and we were happy for him.

Over the next four years, Rick got thinner. I believe the last time I saw him he was only 100 pounds if that. He also started losing his hair. He always kept his hair long, something close to a classic 1980's mullet. When the wind blew, it would expose a large bald area on his head. His wife got bigger. We never saw her in person, but Rick would show us a picture now and then. The last photo I saw with the two of them reminded me of a pencil and a soccer ball.

One morning at work, Rick received a phone call from home. He told us there was a situation at home and he had to leave immediately. His boss heard from Rick in the late afternoon. The phone call Rick received in the morning was his wife in hysterics. She thought she expelled parts of her bowels while relieving herself. There was a bloody mess in the toilet, and she thought her intestines were exposed but still attached. Rick told her to call 911 and drove home at break-neck speed. He and a pair of paramedics arrived at his home within seconds of each other. They discovered that Rick's wife woke up feeling nauseated. She went to the bathroom to relieve herself. She gave a push but felt like something was still tugging on her. She had given birth while defecating. The child was in the toilet, luckily with its head turned upwards. It was covered in blood and feces with its arms and legs curled together, not looking very human. What she thought were her intestines was the umbilical cord extending from her vagina. By the time Rick and the paramedics arrived, she passed the afterbirth and realized what had actually happened. She had no idea she had been pregnant.

A few months after having the baby, Rick announced he was leaving the company. They were moving back to the Midwest to be closer to her family.

Coach!

I used to coach sports. My step-children, Ryan and Sarah, played baseball and soccer. I coached Ryan's little league baseball teams and Sarah's girls soccer. My personal sports activities involved Tae Kwon Do. As a Tae Kwon Do black belt, I would assist the Master during class. During competition season, I also assisted the kids and teens for sparring training. So, I did a lot of coaching and met some interesting kids.

I had a knack for reading the kid's rhythm. I saw it when they would run the bases or swing the bat. Once I identified the patterns of their motion, I tried to optimize their natural rhythm to their intended actions. One of the bigger boys on the baseball team liked to use a heavy bat, probably because he thought a heavier bat was for a larger ball player. Each time he swung his heavy bat, he was about a quarter second too late hitting the ball. I watched him at bat three times only to go down swinging each time. On his fourth time up, I had him use a mid-weight bat. He hit a home run off the first pitch. He went on to be a 'first pitch' batter for the remainder of the season, hitting a double or better each time.

My step-daughter Sarah had a hilarious running style while playing soccer. She ran on her toes. It looked like she was jamming her toes into the ground with each stride along with her elbows sticking way out, barely swinging her arms. She appeared slow and unbalanced when she ran; however, it was her way to zone the field, then with a burst of speed, she would steal the ball from a player or intercept a pass.

Another girl named Stephanie, called Stevie by her teammates, was of average height for an eight year old girl with a long straight ponytail that fell below her waist. She was shy and loved to play the game but lacked the aggression to challenge an opposing player for the ball. Her mother would complain about Stephanie not applying herself and always threatened to end Stephanie's participation on the team. The head coach kept her as a defender where she was marginally capable of preventing advancement of the ball. I could tell that she really wanted to control the ball, but her shyness held back the aggression she needed to stand up to the strikers. As an experiment, I put her in the goalkeeper position. I told her that she was not to let the ball get by her and that she was allowed to run ahead and steal the ball with her hands before the opposing player can kick it. The extra space was all she needed to charge the ball. Not a ball got passed her for a half hour as her teammates and coaches bombarded her with shot attempts on goal. I remember how excited she was after practice, telling her father how well she did. I personally worked with Stevie at every practice on her new role as a goalkeeper. After each practice and game, I would discuss with Stevie how well she was improving; I asked her how she was going to avoid mistakes; and I also talked about how being a goalkeeper can apply to other things outside of soccer. Stevie became the number two goalie for the team.

Another girl liked to play goalkeeper and center-forward. Cathy was bigger than the other girls, and she was the daughter of the other assistant coach. She had a powerful foot and when playing as a striker, she would try to kick too hard. Her stride would break just prior to kicking the ball and she would lose control. She was eager to score and believed kicking as hard as she could guaranteed a goal. It took a while, but I convinced her that assisting a goal was as important as making the goal. When Cathy passed the ball to a teammate, she was perfect every time. She wasn't focused on scoring, so she developed an excellent ability to pass. I told her that unless she was unimpeded to the goal she should pass to Sarah or Vicky or one of the advancing defenders that could make the shot. I also told her that no other girl on the team could kick the ball with as much power as she could, but the other strikers were more accurate. As Cathy racked up assists, her confidence in her kicking grew.

Fast forward 12 years…

One Friday evening, I was walking through the Savannah airport. I had just returned from a business trip to Irvine, California. I was tired and aching from a long, cramped flight. I just wanted to get to my car and go home. I had a 20 minute drive ahead of me.

Midway through the concourse I heard a girl scream, "AAAH! AAAH!" I looked around. About 40 feet in front of me was this girl starting to run in my direction with her arms in the air. I looked behind me, thinking she may have spotted her father or boyfriend.

"AAAH! AAAH!" she yelled. This girl was hot. Beautiful. About five feet nine inches tall. Long raven hair. Big boobs. I'm starting to think this is my lucky day. She was coming straight at me. I thought she was going to jump into my arms and wrap her legs around me.

"Coach! Coach!" she yelled when she was arms-length from me. She wrapped her arms around me in a bear hug. I could not believe what was happening to me. What a crazy way to meet someone, but I was enjoying the hug from the beautiful girl. What was she talking about?

"Coach, it's me. Stevie!" She planted a kiss on my cheek. "Coach, you helped me through so much! I thought about what you told me when I was having hard times…" She said in a semi-sobbing voice as she hugged me tightly.

"It's good to see you Stevie," I said as best I could. We talked in the middle of the concourse for several minutes. A part of me was thrilled to see her and hear about her life. And another part of me enjoyed too much the feel of her young, firm body against mine. I felt so dirty.

Don't Mess with the Swan

I would go to the Pita Pit in Pooler, GA once a week to buy a pita sandwich and return to my office for lunch. The Pita Pit was located on Benton Blvd just south of the Pooler Parkway in a multi-office building shared with a Cricket Wireless store and a few other businesses. Just south of the building was a retention pond for irrigation and rain run-off from the Godley Preserve apartments. The retention pond was about a mile away from the 9/27 runway of the Savannah International Airport. The pond was loaded with migratory ducks and geese all the time. It is surprising the Savannah Airport Commission didn't object to a retention pond location directly in the flight path of aircraft taking off and landing.

On this particular day, there were more than the usual number of cars parked in front of Pita Pit. I was annoyed that I had to park my car around the corner from the front entrance. After getting out of my truck, I moved toward an awning that covered the walkway surrounding the building. The parking lot and the walkway were covered in duck and goose feces, thanks to the adjacent pond. I was about five feet away from the building when I stopped in my tracks because I noticed a swan lying in the shade of the awning. The bird was huge. You don't realize how big a swan is until you are this close to one. It had its feet tucked under him and its head draped over its left wing. The bird was in the classic sleeping swan pose, but this one wasn't sleeping. One eye was open looking right at me. It obviously noticed me before I noticed it. Since it didn't move up to this point, I was curious if it was injured. I slowly stepped toward the swan, and it hissed a warning at me. No problem, I thought. It wants to sleep in peace; I won't bother it.

I turned the corner heading toward the Pita Pit entrance, avoiding the waterfowl shit on the walkway. There was a Pita Pit employee by the door, screwing a water hose onto a spigot. He was wearing a store apron with a nametag, "Toby". Toby was a six and half feet tall black teenager, and by my estimate about 300 lbs.

"Watch your step, sir," he said when he saw me walk toward the door. "There's bird mess everywhere and I's gonna clean it."

"Be careful, there is a swan around the corner," I said. "Don't mess with it."

"A swan, sir?" he said, opening the door for me.

"Thanks. Yes, stay clear of it. They can be mean," I told Toby as I walked in.

"I ain't never seen a swan before," Toby said, and with a curious look on his face, he started walking in the direction of where the swan was resting.

I should have paid better attention to what Toby was saying, but I went to the counter and placed my order. A few minutes later, there was a scream that sounded like it was coming from somewhere outside the building.

"YEEAAAHHH! AAAHH! AAAHH!" someone screamed in a high pitched voice, getting louder and closer.

A big body ran to the door screaming, "AAHH! MAMA!"

It was Toby all disheveled with cuts and scratches on his arms. There was a scratch and a bruise on his face too. He was crying, tears gushing out of his eyes. The cashier ran to him. She asked, "Toby, what happened?!"

"It was so pretty. I just wanted to pet it," Toby sobbed.

"What was pretty, Toby?" the cashier asked.

"The sw-sw-sw... The sw-sw," Toby cried.

"Did you try to pet that swan?" I asked. "I told you not to mess with it."

"Yes, sir. It looked so pretty. I just wanted to pet it. I tried and it attacked me," Toby cried. He didn't understand the hissing coming from the swan meant 'leave me alone.' The swan leapt on him, clawing and biting. Swans have long, sharp claws and barbs on their heels, like rosters do. The swan tore up his arms and bit him on the face and neck.

"I don't know why the swan didn't like me; I just wanted to pet it and maybe feed it. You know like I does with the ducks," Toby said with voice full of innocence and regret.

The cashier hugged Toby as best she could since he was twice her size. "Well Toby, let's just stick to petting ducks and let the swans be."

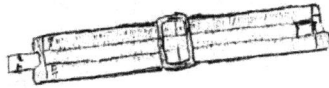

Slide Rule

The professors at Parks College were a unique group of educators. The Parks College of Saint Louis University was (and still is) the Aviation and Engineering college of the university. Parks College was located across the Mississippi River in Cahokia, Illinois – geographically separate from the main campus in the city of St. Louis. The Parks student body population averaged 800. The professors taught students directly and performed all their administrative duties themselves, such as grading and teaching laboratory classes.

Doctor John Rhodes taught three of my Engineering classes: Dynamics, Structural Loads, and Stress. He was a tall, cantankerous man in his 60s with receding gray hair that still contained hints of its original blonde, and thick lensed eyeglasses that slid halfway down his nose. He had an unkempt look, always wearing brown pants, brown shoes, a white or yellow dress shirt without a tie, and a beige sport coat. His most distinguishing features were the lit cigarette that always dangled from his lips and that his right hand was missing its index finger. He was right-handed. If Dr. Rhodes was in a good mood when using his hand to count, the number one was displayed with his hand vertically edge-on. Otherwise, he would use his middle finger.

The Parks legend about Dr. Rhodes was that he invented the aerosol push valve and thus he was worth millions. He frequently said that he was well off. He claimed he was teaching at Parks because he didn't like golf and that he could only spend so much time with his wife.

Classes with Dr. Rhodes usually started ten minutes late. The first half of the remaining class time involved discussions of his upcoming vacation (usually in Boca Raton), topics on news the night before, and the Civil War. The second half of class time was the subject lecture including two examples as work problems he solved on a chalkboard. The lecture always included a few minutes of his disapproval of "those heathen metric units." Dr. Rhodes despised the metric system – he was an imperial system engineer. Regardless of his displeasure, he repeatedly told his class that we should consider ourselves bilingual, as in being fluent with the English and Metric systems of Engineering.

Dr. Rhodes was the only instructor during my college career that took attendance at the beginning of each class. In his initial class of the semester, he informed his students that he smoked during the lectures and if anyone had a problem with that, they could either take the class with a different instructor or sit by a window. He also stated that any student would be guaranteed a passing grade if he or she gifted him a bottle of Royal Salute Scotch. Back in the early 1980s, Royal Salute was $100 per bottle. A few weeks into the semester after reminders of how a bottle of Royal Salute would guarantee a passing grade, we 30 students pooled our money and had a gift-wrapped bottle of Royal Salute waiting on the classroom podium for him. It was the only time I remember seeing Dr. Rhodes smile during class. He was touched and thanked us, but the offer was for a single student. Being magnanimous, he said he would award each student an additional three points on each test grade.

The Engineering classes usually had five or six exams, including the final exam, each semester depending on the instructor. Dr. Rhodes claimed he would give four exams per semester, but we would be lucky if he issued two exams. If you performed badly on the first exam, there was almost no chance to recover your grade with only the final exam remaining.

My second class with Dr. Rhodes was Structural Loads. It was nearly the middle of the semester, and we were about to have our first exam. Half the class was in the student lounge cramming at the last minute before class. Dr. Rhodes' exams were notoriously difficult, so everyone, including me, was very nervous. With less than ten minutes prior to the exam, my calculator died. It was a Texas Instruments TI-55 II that used watch batteries. I nearly panicked. I ran to the bookstore in the student lounge to buy a new set of batteries, but there were none available. I ran back to my classmates as they were packing their backpacks to go take the exam, did anyone have a spare calculator? No luck!

I needed a calculator. I didn't have time to walk back to my apartment to get my roommate's calculator, but there should be one in the Physics Lab! I worked as a teaching assistant in the Physics laboratory, along with two other students, Angus and Harold. I was certain there was a calculator in the storeroom of the lab. I could use the lab calculator for the exam! The lab was located on the opposite side of the campus from the lounge in McDonnell Douglas Hall. I ran through a rain shower to get to the Physics lab only to find a note in the desk drawer that usually housed the calculator:

Borrowed the calculator, my batteries died. Angus

Now I was in a real panic. What was I going to do? It would take too long to perform hand calculations during the exam…maybe there are watch batteries here in the lab? No luck! I opened the calculator drawer again, hoping it would magically reappear. The calculator wasn't there, but I noticed a slide rule under Angus' note. A slide rule! I'm saved!

I ran through the rain again to Assembly Hall for the exam. I felt proud of myself that I knew how to use a slide rule. My father was a draftsman and there were slide rules in the house, but he never had time to show me how to use it. Living across the street was my friend Nick, whose father was an architect. His father showed him how to use a slide rule, and he in turn showed me. A slide rule wasn't as fast as a calculator and I would have to write down progress as I performed calculations, but I felt that I had a fighting chance to complete the exam.

I made it to the classroom as Dr. Rhodes began taking attendance. I sat in my usual seat with pencils, eraser and slide rule ready. Dr. Rhodes tossed a stack of papers to the nearest student and told him to pass it around so everyone received a test. The exams got to me. I took one and passed the remainder to the student sitting next to me. I took a deep breath. Exhaled. I started the first problem.

Using a slide rule is like riding a bike – you don't forget. You might be a little wobbly if it's been a while, but it comes back to you quickly. I repeated the first two or three calculations to convince myself I was using the device correctly. I was humming along, moving the cursor, switching between multiplication and division, using the A and D scales for roots, etc. I was a few calculations into the third exam problem when I felt laser beams drilling into my back. I suddenly felt very paranoid. Cigarette ash fell on my exam paper. I looked over my shoulder to see Dr. Rhodes less than a foot away, glaring down at me!

"What...the hell...are you doing, Hannaway?" Dr. Rhodes asked while puffing on his cigarette.

"Taking the test," I replied.

He extended his right hand toward the slide rule and grunted, an indication that he wanted it. He looked at the slide rule noting the position of the slide and cursor. He handed it back to me. He then looked down at my exam paper. He straightened himself and grunted again making a winding gesture with his hand as if to say "continue."

I did the next calculation on the slide rule, wrote the result on the paper, then looked up at Dr. Rhodes. I also noticed that every student in the classroom was looking at me and the professor, wondering what was going on. Dr. Rhodes grunted again with his hand extended. I gave him the slide rule again. He looked at it. He handed it back to me then grabbed my exam papers.

"Get out, Hannaway!" Dr. Rhodes said loudly.

"What?" I replied with surprise and confusion.

"You heard me," he said as he crumpled my exam in his hands, "Get out."

I slowly got out of my chair. Every student had a look of horror on their faces. Dr. Rhodes had never yelled at any of us before. This was bad. I put on my coat with as much dignity as I could muster, grabbed my book bag and exited the hall.

I stood outside for a while in disbelief. What happened? What did I do? What did I say? I can't fail that exam. Failing one exam was as good as failing the entire class. If I failed that class, my grade point average would take a bad hit. I may have to take an additional semester because the class prerequisites would be out of sync. I couldn't afford another semester. I couldn't believe how badly I just got screwed.

I decided I would go to Dr. Rhodes' office later that day to apologize for everything and anything I could think of and beg to retake the exam. I had two hours to kill before the self-flogging could start, so I went to the student lounge to rehearse my appeal to Dr. Rhodes. My classmates entered the lounge in pairs or threes. They asked what had happened. I replied that I didn't know, I was just as surprised as they were. I asked what Dr. Rhodes did after I left and what his mood was. They said he was his usual self.

I arrived at his office an hour later. Dr. Rhodes shared an office with Dr. Ben Ulrich, who taught Aircraft Design. Unfortunately for me, Dr. Ulrich was also there and there would be a witness to the self-debasing I was about to do. Dr. Rhodes desk was more unkempt than his appearance. There were three pyramids of papers, books and other materials stacked nearly three feet high. There was a fourth stack looking more like a plateau with a large ashtray overflowing with ashes and cigarette butts. Dr. Rhodes was sitting in his office chair with his legs extended over an open desk drawer, reading a magazine with a lit cigarette dangling from his lips.

"Excuse me, Doctor Rhodes? May I have a few minutes of your time," I asked in the humblest voice I could speak.

"Whatchya want, Hannaway?" he replied without looking at me.

"Doctor Rhodes, I am very sorry for what I said and what I did in class today. May I retake the exam? I can't afford to fail this class. I may have to take a year off school to earn enough money to take an addition semester if I get out of sync…"

Dr. Ulrich turned to look in my direction. Obviously, he heard something interesting.

"Why should you retake the exam, Hannaway? You passed it."

"I passed it?" I asked in disbelief.

"Ben, this guy used a slide rule while taking my exam," Dr. Rhodes said looking at Dr. Ulrich with a smile on his face.

Dr. Ulrich chuckled. "That's good," he said, "looks like we have an engineer that knows how to function during a power failure."

"Why were you using a slide rule?" Dr. Rhodes asked. I explained about my calculator dying a few minutes before the exam and finding the slide rule in the Physics lab. I also mentioned learning how to use the device from my neighbor who was an architect. The two professors told me how they fought the use of calculators for exams for a few years, but eventually gave in to keep up with technology.

Dr. Rhodes told me that he would give me a grade between 90 and 100 for the exam and he also insisted that I tell no one of our deal until after I graduated.

Epilogue: Fifteen years later, I was assisting the Savannah Tae Kwon Do Academy's annual yard sale to raise money for the students to travel to Junior Olympics. I was counting the proceeds from the sales and could not find paper or a calculator to do the addition. In the owner's office was an abacus that was used as a decorative piece. I took the abacus to the table with the till and totaled the denominations, moving beads up and down appropriately. I received stares and questions from parents and students alike.

Unusual Business Trip

During my career as a flight test engineer, I've had to do my job in remote, desolate locations; and I've also done my job in five-star places. Once, I had to spend a week at a company facility in Long Beach, CA to test a modification to a US Army GV, also known as a VC-37A. Since this was a military owned airplane, a project engineer from the Special Missions Program Department whose name was Dan, was involved. Another engineer and up-and-coming manager, Lawson, was also on the team.

Dan and I had worked together for the past ten years on the various aircraft certification programs and other follow-on projects. Dan was great to work with and loved to have a good time. Lawson had only been with the company for three years and never traveled on company business before, so this was a good time for Dan and me to have fun at Lawson's expense.

I had lived and worked in the Long Beach area eleven years earlier. Dan, as the project engineer, had been traveling to Long Beach regularly for a few months. Both of us knew the area and what to expect in the 'Southern California Atmosphere.' Lawson had never been to California. We were staying at the Renaissance Hotel in downtown Long Beach near Shoreline Village. Dan and I told Lawson about Shoreline Village and of some of the restaurants and bars during the flight over from Georgia. We also kidded with him about how, as a newbie, all food and beer was on him; and that he had to call in to the Director of Project Engineering to give updates each night.

We arrived at the Renaissance hotel to check-in. The concierge was a short cubby black man with a cherubic face, close-cropped hair and gold rimmed circular "granny" eyeglasses. His skin was a perfect milk chocolate color. He wore what appeared to be a new crisp concierge uniform with a nametag showing 'SEMI.' He was a bit swishy with all his effeminate motions and gestures. He spoke with a lisp as he asked for our information.

"Is you name Sem-eye?" Dan asked.

"No thir, it's Them-mee," Semi replied.

"As in semi-sweet?" I asked. *I don't know why I said it – it was blurted out before I could stop myself.*

"Oh, thir," Semi said placing two fingers against his smiling lips blushing as he peered over the top of his eyeglasses, "Don't you know it."

"Lawson," I said turning to him, "Semi here is going to rock our world. You should come down and see him after you unpack your case."

"I'm at your thervith, thir," Semi replied, looking at Lawson, "any thervith you need."

Lawson had the "deer in the headlights" look, unable to speak. Dan poked him and gestured to follow us. Dan and I had a quiet chuckle between us walking to the elevator.

Later that day, we strode to Yard House Brewery in Shoreline Village for dinner with an additional goal to get Lawson hammered for the night. Our waitress was an attractive girl with a very pale complexion and long black hair that unfurled halfway down her back. She wore a mini-skirt with a revealing, translucent sleeveless blouse showing nothing underneath. Needless to say, she caught our attention.

Right away, Dan had to say something about her appearance. "I really like your outfit."

"Everybody likes it," she replied, "You should see my tips…"

Lawson spit some beer. "Did you say 'your tits'?" he said with high school enthusiasm.

"I'll get another round," she said rolling her eyes as she walked away.

"Don't you kill my fun," Dan said to Lawson. "Or I'll report you to the boss."

"Watch out, that girl can hurt you," I said to Dan. "And I don't want the bar manager throwing us out of here because you abused the waitress," I said to Lawson.

Dan pulled out his cell phone. He announced he was calling his supervisor, the Director of Project Engineering, to give him a status of the day. Earlier he was telling Lawson that after he provides the daily status, he calls again to leave informal messages about how the evening progresses. Lawson called "bullshit" on Dan, saying it was job suicide to leave messages on your boss's voicemail as you got hammered through the night. Dan said that all the project engineers did it because they travel so much, and the director was cool with it. It was a way to let the boss know they were having fun and working hard.

Dan made his first phone call, leaving a straight-forward message about the day. He ended by saying he would call back to discuss what's going on at dinner. He made another phone call, leaving a message describing the waitress in graphic R-rated detail.

It took a while, but Lawson was convinced to call Dan's boss. His first message thanked him for the opportunity to go on this trip. He called a second time leaving a message about the fun night he was having. The subject of the waitress would come up, causing Dan and Lawson to make raucous comments.

When the waitress would approach the table, Lawson would turn around as if speaking on the phone. Dan would eye her up and down with a sick grin. During a refill round when Lawson wasn't at the table, the waitress told Dan and me that she knew what we were doing to Lawson. We told her it was his first business trip. It was all harmless fun and the worst thing that could happen was that Lawson would have a slight hangover in the morning.

Dan asked her if she wanted to play along. Flirt a bit. It would be hilarious to make a pass at Lawson just to see his reaction. He also suggested she make up a story about her. She said she would talk to us when she returned with a fresh round of beer. She also said she didn't have to make up a story.

Lawson returned from the men's room. I was talking into my phone pretending to leave a "less than professional" message to Dan's boss, ending with "Lawson will call you later."

"I have to admit," Lawson said with a burp, "that waitress is looking pretty good. Doesn't seem as intimidating as before." The beer was obviously affecting him.

"Are you sure you want to go there?" I asked Lawson with a teasing connotation in my voice.

"You're not in her league," Dan told him. "Give her a compliment on her looks when she comes back. You'll know if she's interested by the way she looks at you."

That's a crock of shit I thought to myself. The waitress showed no emotion the whole time she served us – she was complete deadpan. But Lawson seemed enthused. He thought there might be something there.

The waitress returned with a tray full of pints of ale. As she placed the glasses on the table, she looked at each one of us directly in the eyes. It felt like she was trying to scan our minds – looking into our souls. It was kind of spooky.

Lawson recovered. "You look incredibly fit. What's your routine to stay in shape?"

"Sex," she replied in complete deadpan. "I bang… I don't know… six times a day."

"Whoa, your boyfriend does it with you six times a day, every day?" Dan asked in disbelief.

"I don't have a boyfriend. I have partners. My parents raised me in a Christian sex cult since I was eleven."

Dan was speechless. I thought Lawson was going to fall off his stool.

"My shift can end in two hours."

She tucked her tray under her arm and walked away. Lawson was feeling uncomfortable. I couldn't resist asking him if he was ready to go there. He had a look of astonishment. He said he wanted to leave. He had enough of the bar and the waitress. It was all too much for him. Dan placed a pile a money on the table.

We walked back to the hotel, talking the entire time about if the waitress was telling the truth and if she really would have had sex with any of us. Lawson was still frazzled when we got to the hotel. We decided to go to the concierge lounge for a final round for the night, plus Dan and I accomplished our mission to get Lawson hammered. One more round couldn't hurt.

Semi found Lawson asleep in the concierge lounge that evening. He helped Lawson back to his room and "tucked him in" for the night. The next morning, the three of us met in the hotel restaurant for breakfast. Lawson was hung over, but that didn't prevent him from going into a rant about Dan and me trying to ruin his life with a sex-crazed waitress and a gay concierge.

Needless to say, he never went on another business trip with us again.

Chinese Buffet

I had a wife that loved snow crab legs. Her sister also loved snow crab legs. Together they could destroy at least a dozen clusters of crab legs. One cluster is enough for me. I enjoy them too, but I don't overindulge. Apparently, they are not alone with this crab leg illness.

Once a month, my wife would insist on going to the local Chinese Buffet restaurant for the "all you can eat" snow crab legs night. Thankfully for me, this was only a once a month torture event. The food at the Chinese Buffet restaurant wasn't that good. Eating there was always an unpleasant ordeal for me.

One night, we went to the restaurant. It was set up in the typical buffet layout: three tables loaded with chafing trays in the center of the floorplan, booths were along the walls, and several tables between the booths and buffet tables. I noticed, as I usually did on crab leg night, that patrons were sitting at the tables rather than the booths. My wife chose a booth, as usual. I thought about telling her that sitting at a table could be more advantageous, but I concluded it wasn't worth the effort.

We helped ourselves to the various dishes offered at the buffet table: sweet and sour pork, pepper beef, egg rolls, fried rice, etc. The crab legs tray was empty. We took our plates back to our booth. We talked about the events of the day while we ate. I noticed a waitress carrying a chafing tray full of crab legs toward the buffet table. I told my wife that a fresh tray of crab legs are available. She smiled and said she would get some in a few minutes. I saw four people descend on the crab legs, then told her that she ought to go now before they are all gone.

Minutes later, she walked over to the buffet table to get her crab legs. She returned with a small plate containing an egg roll.

"The crab legs are all gone," she said with disappointment. She munched on her egg roll as we continued our conversation. Every now and then she would glance over toward the buffet table checking the status of the crab leg dish. I finished what was on my plate. I decided to help myself to more food. At the buffet table, I selected an egg roll along with a spoonful of steamed rice. A waitress appeared with another chafing dish full of hot crab legs. Before she could load the tray onto its stand, a man and woman (assumed husband and wife) sitting at a table across from the crab legs tray leapt to their feet and began pulling clusters of crab legs onto plates. The couple were very obese people and had jammed the waitress against the buffet table as they reach around and over her to get to the food. I walked around the buffet table to the opposite side from the crab legs tray. I reached across, grabbed a cluster of legs, and then made a hasty retreat to the booth.

"A new batch of crab legs came out of the kitchen, but you better get there now. A well-fed couple is camped next to the crab legs and loading up as we speak."

"About time!" my wife said. "I'm getting a few clusters this time!"

As she approached the table, the large couple departed the buffet table with a plate in each hand, loaded with crab legs stacked at least 18 inches high. My wife along with other customers poked around the empty crab leg dish, then looked angrily over to the couple gorging themselves on the hot crab legs.

61

"This is so unfair!" she said when she returned empty handed. "There were only pieces of legs left in the tray!" I broke my cluster, giving her half. "What's wrong with those people? I'm going to complain to the manager."

"What's that going to accomplish?" I replied, "Buffets are first come, first serve. When the management realizes they won't make a profit tonight, they may say something."

"Well, we paid for a buffet meal just like they did. I'm entitled to eat crab legs too!"

All eyes were watching the obese couple eating their crab legs. In less than five minutes, they ate all the crab meat, leaving broken legs shells on their table. A disgusted waitress scooped the shucks into a large bowl as the couple helped themselves to more food at the buffet. I watched the man gather all the pieces of beef out of the peppered beef tray, leaving the tray full of bell pepper halves and quarters. The woman did the same thing to a shrimp tray – collecting all the shrimp and leaving the vegetables and mushrooms. Looking around the restaurant, I could see that the other patrons were displeased with the situation. People were glaring at the couple and occasionally pointed at them during their conversations.

Another tray of crab legs came out of the kitchen as the couple were feasting on the beef and shrimp. They leapt out of their seats like a deer being shot by a high powered rifle, leaving their half-eaten food on their table to horde the fresh crab legs onto four dishes. My wife and others bolted toward the buffet table but were unable to get to the crab legs because the couple were using all four serving thongs. Their large girth was also a limiting factor. I heard my wife say something about letting others get a chance for crab legs to which the woman replied, "First come, first serve."

My wife came back to the booth very angry. I saw some folks walk from the buffet table straight to the exit. Maybe they already paid or did a "dine and dash," I don't know. She said the couple took the serving thongs with them to their table. She continued complaining. We had been at the restaurant for almost two hours; I was ready to go, but my wife was adamant to have crab legs even if it meant staying until closing time. I had to take control of the situation.

I walked into the kitchen which immediately prompted the head waitress to come after me. She began to tell me that I was not allowed in the kitchen, but I told her I wanted to propose something in private. I offered her ten dollars to secretly notify me before the next batch of crab legs are ready to be served. I said that I wanted to let my wife and others get a chance to have some crab legs. She took the money and politely asked that I return to my table. About five minutes later, the waitress came over to our booth with a sinister smile on her face handing us two serving thongs. I told my wife that crab legs were coming.

I walked to the obese couples table, standing between them and the buffet table. My wife positioned herself at the ready. I leaned over to them, asking if they had plenty to eat and if there was anything special I could get for them. While I talked, the cook came out with the crab legs. The couple tried to get out of their seats, but I blocked them from moving while my wife helped herself to the crab legs. I thanked the couple for their time, turned and grabbed the plate my wife filled with crab legs.

The couple got up, lunging to the crab legs, but my wife turned and said, "Oh no you don't! You will sit down and let others have a turn!"

My wife began to stack clusters on to another plate. The man attempted to reach around her, but she knocked the serving thong out of his hand and told him to sit down. She then addressed the remaining patrons in the restaurant, "Does anyone else want crab legs before these vultures get to them?"

Three people approached with plates in hand. My wife served them clusters of crab legs. Afterward, she used a pair of serving thongs to damage the remaining crab legs in the tray. That didn't stop the obese couple. When my wife left the buffet table, they descended on the chafing tray collecting all the damaged scraps of legs. She happily worked her way through the clusters of crab legs, resuming the conversation we started hours ago.

When we left the restaurant, the obese couple were the last patrons there. The waitress was telling them that the last call for crab legs was with the last tray from the kitchen.

My wife relived the whole encounter while I drove home. "I put them in their place," she said. The only thing I could think to say was that I didn't want to go back to that Chinese buffet again.

At the Supermarket II

Large grocery chain stores nowadays have full service eat-in delis. Back in the 1980's, they were almost non-existent. So, it was an awkward sight to see someone eating in the store while grocery shopping. I recall being in a Ralph's store in Long Beach, CA witnessing two girls eating while in line at the checkout.

This was back in the days before self-checkout and debit cards – purchases were cash or check only. Usually, the store checkout took up to half the time you spent in the grocery store. I was fourth in line with my shopping cart. Ahead of me were two fat girls in their late teens or early twenties. Both were complaining about how hungry they were and the long wait in line for checkout. They were very annoying. One girl pulled a magazine off the rack, flipped through pages threatening to open a bag of Cheetos. The second girl said she wasn't going to wait anymore and proceeded to open a carton of vanilla ice cream. Back then, ice cream came in a foldable thin wax-coated cardboard container. Ice cream in plastic tubs with lids wouldn't become a regular container for another 10 years. She dug her fingers into the ice cream lifting a fistful of vanilla and shoved it in her mouth. The other girl opened the Cheetos and literally raised the bag over her head and chewed the Cheetos puffs as they fell into her mouth. The patrons in line were staring in disbelief. The cashier was too busy processing a customer's check to see what was happening.

In less than 90 seconds, the one girl had devoured the quart of vanilla ice cream, including unfolding the container and licking the residual ice cream off the cardboard. When they were done feasting, both girls tried hiding the evidence under their purses on the bottom of their cart. When it was their turn for checkout, all they had on the conveyer belt was a package of stick butter and a head of lettuce. The cashier asked if their cart was empty, and the girls claimed there was nothing else in the cart. When the cashier asked about the ice cream and chips, the girls denied it despite one girl having melted vanilla ice cream and the other girl with a dusting of orange powder on their mouths and fingers. The patrons in line, including me, tattled that they ate the food no more than 30 seconds ago. The girls raised hell about being accused of something they didn't do. They threw the lettuce and butter at those of us in line and told the cashier to "fuck off" and stormed out of the store.

Epilogue: A few weeks later, several grocery stores had grainy black and white photos of the two girls taped to the entrances with either **THIEF** *or* **NOT WELCOME IN THIS STORE** *in big bold font. The ice cream and Cheetos pilfering had become a regular activity in the surrounding neighborhood supermarkets.*

Lightning

Sometimes in life, one's actions or experience causes a significant change to the company that employs you. In the 20 years I worked at Gulfstream Aerospace Corporation, there are many things and people I influenced through my actions and accomplishments. There is one thing that changed the whole company…

In 2000, the Flight Test department was in between major flight test programs, the GV and GV-SP. The organization was downsized in 1999 and now was slowly ramping up to the desired headcount. The Flight Test Engineering group was a small team, spread into two trailers on the east side of the facility. All the engineers were in one trailer, designated Trailer 36. Next to 36 attached by a wooden walkway was Trailer 8 whose only occupants were the Director (Ben) and his administrative assistant (Hannah).

The summer weather in coastal Georgia is always extreme. Extreme sunshine. Extreme heat. Extreme humidity. Extreme storms. On one particular summer day, a thunderstorm started in the early afternoon and was continuously fed energy from winds and moisture coming in off the coast. It rained hard with rolling thunder and lightning.

I was in my office analyzing flight data. The rain pelting the roof of Trailer 36 was not distracting me at all. Neither was the thunder. I was wearing headphones, listening to music while immersed in the analysis. Occasionally there would be sky to ground lightning reminding me to save my data in case there was a power surge.

I reached a point in the analysis where I needed to print a few charts. The printer was in Trailer 8. I walked out of my office, down a very short hallway to the trailer exit. Three quick strides across the wet wooden walkway, I reached for the doorknob to Trailer 8...

...I was on my back looking up at two people that were looking down at me with the sound of screaming behind them. Here is their version of what happened...

Dick Dalton was in Trailer 8 having just completed a meeting with Ben, the Director of Flight Test. Dick didn't want to deal with the rain, so he called his plane captain to send someone in a vehicle to pick him up. Dick was in the vestibule area of the trailer talking with Hannah while waiting for his ride. Hannah, an elderly black lady, was clearly upset by the thunder and lightning and was muttering about what to do.

BANG!!! Lightning struck the trailer! It shook as the power went out. A large object surrounded in a dark blue electric aura flew into the trailer a few feet off the ground across the vestibule, impacting the wall opposite the door. The object slid down the wall behind the printer. Hannah screamed. Dick ran to the printer. Ben ran out of his office. Dick saw it was me and pulled me away from the wall as Ben moved the printer.

Dick was yelling down at me, "Dennis, you OK?!"

Ben excitedly asked, "Dennis, can you move?!"

Hannah screamed, "AAH! AAH! HE DEAD! HE DEAD!" and wet herself.

Piecing it all together...

It had been raining hard for several hours. The wooden walkaway between the trailers was completely soaked by rainwater. Each trailer was a single-wide office style trailer with aluminum siding. There was a power pole between the trailers with elevated power cables supplying electricity to each trailer. Each trailer had a single grounding cable attached to a stake.

The paint hangar, approximately 80 feet away from the Flight Test trailers, was impacted by the main lightning bolt. A finger bolt made contact with the trailer at the moment I opened the door. The doorknob and the wooden walkway were wet, so when the lightning struck I became an electrical conductor for the circuit and was thrown across the trailer.

I tried to sit up. Dick was on one side trying to help me get my shoulders off the floor while Ben was on the other side trying to keep me lying down.

"AAAAAAHHH! HE DEAD!" Hannah continued to scream.

"Look Hannah! He's not dead," Dick said.

"Hannah! Call Medical! Now!" Ben insisted. Hannah was in more shock than I was. She stood there whimpering, bouncing with her arms flailing. Ben went to her and got her to sit down. He called Medical himself.

"Dennis, how are you feeling? Do you hurt anywhere?" Dick asked.

"I'm ok," I said. Looking around I noticed the hole in the wall behind the printer. There was a mild ringing in my ears. The palm of my right hand was red but there didn't seem to be any pain. The medical team, Leticia and Monica from the "Nurses Station" showed up in their Dodge mini-van. By now, the entire complement of Flight Test Engineering was in Trailer 8 standing around me asking questions. A few people helped me to my feet. The nurses wanted me to sit on an office chair and they would roll me on the walkway to the mini-van. I was starting to get annoyed with all the unnecessary attention. Let me walk to the mini-van. But why was I getting in the van anyway? I just wanted to resume what I was doing before I was thrown into a wall.

Leticia explained that it was a workplace incident and I need to be cleared medically to do anything. They drove me to the medical trailer and performed an electro-cardiogram. The data was sent to my primary care physician, and I was cleared. By that time, I was feeling worn out. I decided to go home.

I rested for about two hours feeling no better. I thought maybe if I went to that night's Tae Kwon Do session, I'll start to feel normal again. Exercise was probably what I needed. Twenty minutes into the Tae Kwon Do session, I felt an intense burning sensation in my side, about the size of a baseball. It lasted two or three minutes, then faded away. Ten minutes later, it started again but between my shoulder blades. The on-off burning cycles continued through the night, each time occurring in a different location on my body. By morning, I was back to normal.

Gulfstream conducted a safety investigation into the incident. They installed a Thor Guardian lightning detection alerting system around the facility within weeks. The summer weather in Savannah would cause the lightning alerts to go off several times a day. Each time the alert sounded, I thought it was because of me. Last time I checked (thirteen years after the incident), a black handprint remained on the doorknob of Trailer 8.

I Just Wanted Time To Myself

I lived in the high desert of the Antelope Valley in California in the early 1990s. I worked as a Flight Test Engineer (FTE) for Douglas Aircraft Company, and I rarely had a Saturday off. If the test airplanes were not flying on Saturday, then as an FTE you were analyzing data or preparing flight cards or requesting data or something.

One Saturday came along, and I did not have to work. Two days earlier, I realized that I was able to have a Saturday away from work. I sure didn't want to do household chores or have to repair something, as what usually happens on my short weekends. I had a hundred scenarios in my mind of what I could do: drive to LA for a Dodger game; maybe go to Saddleback Butte Park; go to the movies... Then it hit me – fishing! I hadn't been fishing in years! A relaxing three or four hours fishing on my own would be a perfect Saturday activity.

Elizabeth Lake is a lake located in the Leona Valley within the San Gabriel Mountains. It is a beautiful lake surrounded with pine trees and the cliffs of the surrounding valley. The main road through the town of Elizabeth Lake was on the north side of the lake. A small number of homes were located on the south side of the lake with only two or three homes on the lakeshore. It was a 40 minute drive from my house.

Saturday morning, I began preparing for the trip to Elizabeth Lake. I dug for worms in the yard, making it look like I was attempting to transplant a shrub. When no one was in the garage, I got my fishing pole and tackle box and put the equipment in the back of my truck. When my wife was in the bathroom, I made a sandwich as fast I as could. Grabbed some chips, bottled water, a few cans of beer. I packed the food and beverages in a small cooler while in the garage hiding behind the washing machine. I loaded the cooler into the truck, then snuck around the house into the back yard to get a folding yard chair, making sure the kids didn't notice. I had everything I needed packed into my truck. As I was getting in my vehicle, I had a last minute thought to bring Sally our Golden Retriever with me. Sally would love the lake and the chance to run around.

I called for the dog but rather than seeing Sally trot up to the truck, my wife appeared around the corner.

"Where are you going?' she asked.

Damn! I'm caught! I really wanted the time to myself, and I was hoping to escape unnoticed, then ask forgiveness when I returned. Now I'm caught and she's about to ask me to fix something or do something that will take all day or make me take her and the kids to the mall. My fishing trip was about to slip away on my only Saturday off work in months. I'm going to have to tell her what I'm going to do and ask her to understand my desire.

"I'm going fishing. I'm taking Sally with me," I said. "I'll be back this afternoon."

"Oh cool!" she said, "we've never gone fishing before. Come on kids! Dad's taking us fishing!"

I felt like I was punched in the gut. I really wanted to spend a few hours on my own relaxing. Just three hours of not being a husband or a dad. I sighed – accepted the new self-invitees to the situation.

"Honey, you can grill us hot dogs for lunch too," my wife volunteered. "We can have a picnic!"

I pulled the cooler out of the truck and handed it to my wife. I asked her to load the cooler with all the food and beverages that she and the kids want to take for a picnic.

"Hey Dad? Can I have my own fishing pole?"

"Dad, will you play Frisbee with me?"

"I'm bringing my soccer ball."

Sigh. More to pack.

Thirty minutes later, I had the other fishing pole, three more chairs, blankets, the large cooler, a small "Smokey Joe" Weber grill, charcoal, assorted toys and Sally the dog loaded in the back of my S-15 Jimmy. As I drove to Elizabeth Lake, the kids talked about the fish they were going to catch. They had a long list that included sharks, whales, jellyfish, turtles and alligators. I didn't have the heart to tell them there were no saltwater fish in the freshwater lake. Or that turtles and alligators weren't fish.

When I pulled into the parking area at the lake, all my passengers bolted out of the truck leaving me to unpack everything. Even Sally the dog was gone. I unloaded the folding chairs and carried them to a large tree. I knew my wife was going to want to sit in the shade, so best to claim a spot right away. She immediately unfolded the chair and sat down reading a magazine. She wasn't going to help. The kids were running along the lakefront; Sally was chasing them. After four more roundtrips to the truck, I had everything unloaded. My wife was occupied with her magazine and the kids were not around – I sensed it was a good time to start fishing. Maybe I could hide behind a patch of tall grass for a short while and get some quality time.

At the edge of the lake, I began preparing my pole for the bait. Sally came to me while I was tying the hook on the line. She looked at what I was doing inquisitively with her ears perked up and head cocked. I rubbed her head and ears and told her she was a good girl. Sally then waded into the lake to cool off and drink some water. It was a hot day. I washed my hands in the lake to remove as much dog scent as I could before handling the bait when a couple around my age began setting up their camp only 12 feet away from where I was working with my fishing equipment. A group of Canadian geese swimming in the middle of the lake caught Sally's attention and she began swimming as fast as she could with a bark or two toward the geese. The couple disrobed as I checked the integrity of the knot for my hook. The girl was wearing a green thong bikini. She had an incredible figure and was successfully distracting me from what I was supposed to be doing.

"Hey Dad, Can I help you with the worm?" Ryan appeared out of nowhere. He was standing to my right as I was trying to find a worm in a container of dirt.

"Sure, Ryan," I said glancing at the thong bikini and handed him the container, 'Find a worm."

He handed me a worm. The bikini girl was bending over in my direction adjusting her blanket. I impaled the worm on the hook. "Awesome!" Ryan said as the worm wriggled. I showed him where to impale the worm a second time. I held the hook steady as Ryan attempted to hook the worm and the bikini girl, now bending over in the opposite direction, provided me a view of green butt-floss. The view was burning its image into my mind.

"Is it ready, Dad?" Ryan's question brought me back to reality.

"Yes, it is," I replied. We took a few steps closer to the lake. After casting the line, I propped the pole up using a twig. Ryan wanted to cast but I told him that I brought another pole for him to use. He went to our picnic site to get it.

"Oh look! That's so cute!" The bikini girl was standing pointing into the lake. Sally had caught up to the geese and they were attempting to swim away. Sally barked at the geese while she swam. The geese were flapping their wings to assist their getaway speed causing water splashes and making noise.

Ryan returned with a bamboo cane pole. He watched me intently as I checked the line integrity on the hook. I glanced at the bikini girl; she was sitting on her blanket. Ryan searched for a worm in the bait container and eventually found one as I watched the bikini girl lay back, pillowing her head on a rolled towel.

While I was hooking the worm and watching the bikini girl simultaneously, Sarah began pounding the first fishing pole into the lake WAP! WAP! WAP! telling me she was killing the worm for me. Ryan leapt toward his sister, cane pole in hand, and ripped the hook (and worm) into my hand. Sally had swum back to shore and began shaking herself right next to the bikini girl and her boyfriend.

"I'm getting hungry. When are you going to light the grill?" my wife called from her chair.

I tried to get the hook out of my hand as Ryan led me to his sister. I got the pole away from Sarah telling her the worm is supposed to stay alive. Both poles needed new worms now. Then while holding my bleeding hand, I approached the bikini girl and her boyfriend apologizing for Sally. The water splashing on the bikini girl made her cold in a blazingly obvious manner and I was doing my best, but failing horribly, not to notice. The boyfriend was saying something, probably bitching about my dog interrupting their tan, but I couldn't make out what he said. The bikini girl laughed saying it was ok and cradled Sally's wet head in her hands. That caused Sally to dig her head into the girl's chest, successfully releasing a large breast from her bra. Thankfully, the girl laughed and adjusted her top as she got up. She extended her hand and introduced herself and her boyfriend. I apologized again. Sarah resumed killing the worm. WAP…WAP…WAP.

"I'm getting hungry!" my wife said again with her head in her magazine.

I wallowed in misery for a minute. My relaxing fishing trip turned into a test of my commitment to my family. A part of me wanted to take the bikini girl and Sally, get in my truck and ride to Arizona. But then Ryan said he would help me with the grill, and I returned mentally to my family. Now I needed to keep the lighter fluid away from Ryan or he may burn up the recreation area.

I eventually got the grill lit. I also corralled the kids and the dog into a somewhat controlled area and quickly hooked new worms on the poles. I placed hot dogs on the grill then noticed one of the poles twitching. I ran to the pole, pulled on the line setting the hook into a fish. I began reeling in the fish as it put up a good fight. Suddenly I had a lot of unneeded help.

"Dad! Let me catch the fish!" Ryan cried.

"No let me!" Sarah yelled.

I handed the reel to Ryan instructing him how to reel the line. Sarah insisted on holding the pole while her brother turned the reel. I kept a hand on the pole otherwise it would have flown out of their hands. The fish gradually approached the lakeshore, then Sally noticed the fish splashing around in the water and decided it was her turn to help. She ran into the lake and proceeded to chomp at the fish. Both kids yelled at Sally to leave the fish alone.

"Honey, the hot dogs are burning!"

"I'm busy!" I yelled back.

I grabbed the fish out of the water. I started to get the hook out of its mouth when the events of the previous 20 minutes started all over again. WAP! WAP! WAP! Sarah was killing the worm on the cane pole again. Ryan pulled the other pole at the moment I got the hook out of the fish only to hook my hand again.

"It's burning!!"

"Deal with it!" I replied.

Sally trotted out of the lake and shook herself all over the bikini girl and the boyfriend again.

"Stop fucking around and do something about this burning grill!"

I apologized to the bikini girl yet again but this time both were pissed off. I walked over to my wife, took the can of Coke out of her hand and dumped the contents on the burning hot dogs. I then grabbed a can of beer and walked away.

I needed to walk for a while. I walked to the northern side of the lake, then turned to walk back. I was thinking that I'll just pack everything and everyone back into the truck and go home. I was halfway back to our picnic site, and I noticed Sally laying down under a tree. Looked like a good idea to me. I went over to sit beside her and noticed a lady on a stool with an easel. It looked like she was sketching and painting on a canvas mounted on the easel.

"Sorry. I didn't see you there," I said, "I'll get her out of the way."

"No, please don't," the lady replied. "She's OK. She's very beautiful."

I thanked her for complimenting my dog. I found a shady spot closer to where my wife and the kids were sitting. I was feeling drained of energy, maybe I would take a nap.

I was awakened by my wife. She handed me a burnt hotdog and a beer. I mumbled a thank you and proceeded to eat a burnt but sweet tasting hot dog. When I finished, Sarah came over asking if we could go home. They had packed the truck and were ready to go. The kids talked about catching the fish as I drove home. Their story gathered embellishments of how the fish fought both of them as they reeled it in and how Sally helped.

"Dad?" Sarah asked.

"Yeah?"

"Thanks for taking us fishing. It was real fun."

Epilogue:

Several weeks after the excursion to Elizabeth Lake, I was in the Antelope Valley Mall with the family. One of the kiosks in the mall had several paintings and lithographs by a local artist – the lady with the easel. I saw a beautiful painting of Sally laying under a large shade tree with the lake in the background. It was in a nice frame and had a price tag in excess of $500 with SOLD written on it. The lady I met at the lake saw me and said hello. I mentioned the dog in the painting was my dog. She told me that was correct, and that Sally was a wonderful subject for her art. I joked that I should have asked a modelling fee for Sally. The lady laughed. She said that she couldn't pay a modelling fee but gave me a full-sized lithograph of the painting in an identical frame as a gift.

Joe

I began practicing Tae Kwon Do as an adult in my mid-thirties. I really got into it. I would go to the do-jang three times a week, participating in two classes a night. It was an incredible challenge, especially being nearly seven feet tall. The quickness and agility needed for the Korean style of foot and hand fighting is an antithesis for a giant sized person like myself. I participated in tournaments and won many medals as a colored belt competitor in poomse and sparring categories. As a first degree black belt, I won the Georgia State Tae Kwon Do Championships for 'executive senior heavyweight' men, or in plain terms a male over 35 years of age and over 185 pounds. I won the championship for four consecutive years.

My friends and co-workers knew I was doing Tae Kwon Do. Occasionally, I would show a medal I won in a tournament from the previous weekend. Frequently I would get questions like "have you had to use your fighting skills in real life?"

One weekend I was visiting my girlfriend who lived in Sandy Springs, Georgia. She loved to shoot pool. Every time I visited, we would go to a sports bar called "Whiskers" that was near her condo. Whiskers had three pool tables and every Friday and Saturday night there was a band playing live music. I cannot recall a time we went to

Whiskers and it was not full to capacity of patrons eating, drinking, playing pool or darts, video games, or out on the dance floor enjoying themselves. On this particular night, two of her friends from work accompanied us.

I could be rated as a slightly above average pool player. Some nights I'm hot; other nights not too bad. My girlfriend was an average player – she just loved to shoot pool in a bar and socialize with friends. One of her coworkers, Pavel, was a good player. He could control a table for a while. The other coworker, Joe, was a pool shark.

Joe was less than five and a half feet tall and barely 120 pounds. He was a meek looking guy with coke bottle glasses and would always wear a light jacket regardless of the temperature. Joe was a practical joker amongst his friends and was known to have a vicious streak. When I first met Joe, my girlfriend told me that he paid for his college education by playing pool for money on the weekends. I shot pool against Joe a few times in the past and he was the best pool player I had ever seen.

On this night, the four of us played against each other as partners for about an hour, drinking beer (except my girlfriend, she usually didn't drink), having a good time. Feeling spirited, I covered my hand in chalk and grabbed my girlfriend's ass, leaving a white handprint on her black denim pants. She wondered why everyone was smiling at her. Occasionally a patron would put a quarter on the table to reserve the right to play the next game, but my girlfriend would ask that they wait for two more games, then we would open the table. My girlfriend and Pavel decided to take a break from the game, so Joe and I played. Joe racked the balls, and I broke the rack; then with a surprising bit of luck I proceeded to run the table. My running the table was witnessed by a lot of guys waiting to reserve our table. Joe quickly racked the balls and placed a five dollar bill on a bumper telling me, "It's yours if you could run the table again."

I broke the rack sinking two balls then missed the third. It was now Joe's turn, and he sank all his balls followed by the eight ball for the win. One of the guys watching our match approached the table with quarters in hand ready to join the competition.

"I'll play you for five bucks," the guy said as he loaded quarters into the pool table.

"Okay, rack 'em please," Joe replied.

Joe broke the rack sinking two striped balls. He sank another but his next shot missed the pocket. The newcomer sank a ball, then missed. The match continued back and forth between the two players in a sink-a-ball-then-miss pattern for a few rounds. I could see that they were trying to downplay their abilities to each other as if trying to convince the other that he could win. The match got down to each player with a single ball remaining and it was Joe's turn. He sank his stripe ball, then easily shot the eight ball into a corner pocket.

"Thanks," Joe said as he pocketed the money. Another guy stepped up with quarters and said, "Play for another five?"

"Okay," Joe said as he finished his beer.

This match didn't last as long as the previous one. By the time it was Joe's fourth time up, he won the game. And the pattern continued through five other players. Joe was up $30 and had bought three rounds of beer for me, Pavel and himself. The first guy that Joe played returned to the table. He had played at a different table, while watching the last two competitors at Joe's table.

"I'm warmed up now. How about a game for $10?" he asked as he put four quarters into the pool table.

"Okay, rack 'em," Joe said with a verbal inflection that hinted he was buzzed. He should have been buzzed because he already had four rounds of beer.

The more you shot pool with Joe, the more comfortable he would feel about coaching you how to play. Add the beer and the money on the table, Joe could really come off as arrogant with his unwanted coaching. If you sank a ball after he provided advice, he would rub it in with, "See? Wasn't that easy."

During the $10 match, Joe started giving unsolicited advice to his opponent. This guy was not pleased and at first ignored Joe, but eventually told Joe to "keep it to himself." That was the wrong thing to say to Joe because he promptly ran the rest of the table.

"Thanks for the game," Joe said as he pocketed the money ordering another round of beer.

"Double or nothing?" the loser asked with attitude.

"Fuck that," Joe said in a burp and a slight stagger, "Fifty!"

"You're on!"

Remarkably, the more Joe drank, the better he played. Instead of giving advice during this $50 game, Joe did trick shots and won in only three rounds.

I leaned over to Pavel, "After a $50 loss, this guy should walk away. Joe is looking drunk." And he was. He had a perpetual smile on his face, and he was squinting his eyes. Joe also had a pronounced stagger in his walk. He laughed at everything.

"Don't count on it," Pavel said, "Joe found a pigeon. He's going to clean this guy."

"Again!" the opponent demanded.

"Hundred!" Joe said.

"You're on!"

Joe and his opponent went at it again for $100. As I watched Joe play, I also looked around to see what trouble my girlfriend was getting into. She had been playing at a different table. Three leather clad bikers with shaved heads were playing at her table and it looked like she was doing more than just shooting pool. She was lecturing. She held her pool cue in her left hand with the butt of the cue on the floor. Her right index finger was extended and was gently poking the tallest biker in the chest. He had an intense look on his face as he glared down at her. His two friends were beside him laughing. The side of my girlfriend's ass with the white chalk handprint was facing me. It was still as pronounced as when I first put it there. That told me that no one tried to place their hand on her ass or waist, so her lecturing wasn't about the biker being inappropriate.

"Wow, this is so easy!" Joe defeated his opponent in two rounds and this guy was losing his composure. I was sure he was thinking "how could I lose to this drunk asshole runt."

"Why don't you let someone else play," Joe asked as he placed the bills on his growing wad of cash.

"Fuck you," he said as he stormed off.

One of his friends stepped up. "No money, I just want to play for fun," he said. So, he and Joe played a game that lasted about 10 minutes. They player that lost over $200 came back watching most of the game. Joe intentionally dragged the game out and the guy that lost a lot of money thought Joe was finally vulnerable.

"Alright, you're going to lose," he said as he jammed quarters into the table slots. "Three hundred dollars!" as he stacked 20 dollar bills on the table bumper.

"Okay, I'll double or nuthin' you," Joe slurred, "if you win, I'll pay you $600."

"Oh, you're fucking on," the guy said as he racked the balls.

The game got started. I wasn't keen on the tension in the air. Looking around, I noticed my girlfriend was still near the bikers. She was leaning over her pool table taking a shot as the bikers drank beer and looked on. Pavel was sitting at the bar playing video poker. Joe was now shooting one handed, keeping his left hand in his pocket. Even one-handed, Joe was undefeatable, making each shot look as if only luck allowed him to sink the balls.

"Shit!" his opponent yelled as he slammed the butt of his cue against the floor. Joe took the cash. He walked to a stool and began counting the big roles of $20 bills. He was clearly drunk. The guy that lost the money tried to take the cash out of Joe's hand, but Joe pulled away nearly falling off the stool. I was over to Joe's side in two strides.

"Lay off. He won it fairly," I said over the music.

"This asshole has been taking my money all night. There's no way he could be so lucky. I'm taking it back," the angry pooler player announced.

"Don't go there," I said. "You're gonna get hurt."

"I'll play you again so you can get your money back," Joe slurred, "I'll set up the table. You got five hundred?"

The guy was incensed. "What do you mean five hundred? Just put your money on the table."

"Five hundred in case you blow it. There should be something in it for me," Joe said.

As they negotiated what I hoped would be the last match, my girlfriend came over with the bikers. The three bikers each had a beer in hand. The tallest one, who I assumed was their leader, had a look of frustration on his face. "What the hell did she get into" raced through my mind.

"Hey babe, this is Scorpio," she said. "His wife has cancer; that's why he shaved his head. He looks tough but he's really a sweetheart. Tonight is his one night out this month. His sister-in-law is taking care of his wife tonight so he can go out with his friends. Isn't that sweet? I asked him to show you his bike…"

"Hey Scorpio," I said extending my hand. "Hold on a moment. There could be a situation here."

Joe and his opponent appeared to have settled on their next bet. His irate opponent was collecting money from his friends. There was incentive: Joe put up his entire winnings versus their $500.

"I don't know how he does it," Pavel said as he joined us.

"What's going on?" my girlfriend asked.

"Joe reeled this guy in all night and he's too stupid to walk away. Joe suckers him in to betting more and more. Joe is really fucked up now. He could blow this one."

Pavel gestured over to Joe who was racking the balls one ball at a time with his right hand because he was bracing himself with his left. He was rocking side to side as he racked. As he positioned the rack on the table, his opponent approached, along with his friends, holding the money in his hand.

"Where's your money?" the guy asked.

Joe pulled the rolled bills out of his jacket pocket.

"Here's mine. Let's have this lady hold the money. She'll give it to you when you win."

He handed his cash to my girlfriend and gestured to the guy to do the same. My girlfriend took their money and began to count it.

"Don't give it to him unless he wins," Joe said to her.

"Hide it," Pavel told her.

"Where?"

"In your bra," he replied.

My girlfriend had 36C boobs, but she was wearing a thin, tight turtleneck sweater. There was no way she could hide all that cash in her sweater and be discrete. I placed my fingers between her belly and the waistband of her jeans, pulled the jeans away and moved the hand with the money toward her panties.

"Stuff it in there in case something goes down, then go hide it in your car," I told her.

Joe took two sideways steps and plopped down on a low back stool with wheels. His momentum rolled him against a table.

"Go ahead and break big guy," Joe taunted from his stool.

85

"This is going to be your loss," the guy said. He broke the rack, sinking a solid colored ball. As he lined up for his next shot, Joe started to laugh drunkenly. The guy missed his shot.

Joe tried to standup but could not get himself off the stool, so he rolled the stool over to the pool table traversing the six foot distance as he giggled. He lined up his shot still sitting in the stool, then sank the ball with a one-handed shot. Joe laughed hysterically. He rolled on the stool to make the next shot, sinking the ball in the pocket, one handed again. The bikers were clapping and yelling "Whoa!" as Joe put on a show. I glanced quickly at Pavel. He looked at me with the "I don't like this" look on his face. My girlfriend was smiling and bouncing up and down.

"Go Joe!" she yelled.

"Damn, he's good," Scorpio said. "I've been watching all night. The drunker he gets, the better he plays."

"Yeah," I replied. "But he should have stopped hours ago. I may need back up. Can you help me out if something goes down?"

"Gotchya covered" Scorpio nodded.

Joe sank all the striped balls one-handed from the rolling stool, laughing the whole time he shot. The opponent and his friends yelled "Shit!" or "Fuck!" each time Joe sank a ball, getting angrier and angrier. Joe finally lined up the eight ball and took his shot. The eight ball was inches away from going into a corner pocket giving Joe the win when one of the guy's friends knocked the eight ball off the table with his pool cue.

"No fucking way! Where's the girl with the money?" the guy's friend asked. Joe's opponent reached over to Joe, intending to lift him off the stool by the jacket. I strode between Joe and the irate guy and his equally irate friends. Pavel bossed my girlfriend away from the impending fracas toward the nearest exit.

"No way asshole," I said. "He won. You and your friends should have walked away hours ago. Leave him alone."

"He didn't win," the guy said, "He missed."

"Don't give me that crap. Your friend interfered. You lose!"

"I want my money!"

"If you won't accept defeat, then game's not over. Got to have a winner if you want to collect."

"Fine have him rack again!"

"He's done," I said, "he's not playing anymore."

"Sure, you're playing in his place?"

"Yeah, but something of my choice." While I was having this exchange with the loser, I was making myself as intimidating as possible. I was standing at my near seven foot height, drawing my shoulders back, deepening my voice and looking as stern as I could.

"Fuck you," the guy said.

"Then you forfeit the money," I demanded. "Get lost!"

"I want my money!" he demanded in return.

"Then you'll have to fight me for it," I replied. "Come on, let's go." I walked toward the back exit.

"You think you can take all of us?"

"Maybe not all at the same time. I'll take you out one at a time. Come on boys, time to get hurt!"

"You're talking real big, mister. We'll kick the shit out of you."

"Hell, I'll take two of you at once. Hey Scorpio! You and your friends make sure all four of these assholes don't jump me at once? I'll take them two at time."

"Got you covered, dude!" Scorpio replied.

Scorpio's reply distracted the assholes. I hooked kicked the bottles of Bud Light from the hands of the two nearest assholes. I grabbed a third asshole's hand holding a bottle of Bud Light and hammered the top of the bottle with my fist. The bottle shattered in his hand, cutting his palm. One down.

"You boys are about to be schooled by the Georgia Tae Kwon Do champion," Pavel yelled.

"That don't scare me."

"Dude, earlier today he did a demonstration where he dispatched two guys at once. He knows what he's doing. And if he gets pissed off, he doesn't hold back."

"Come on, let's go," I said. Scorpio and his friends started herding the four assholes toward the nearest door. While this was going on, my girlfriend wheeled Joe out of the bar to her car. She poured him into the car with the help of a waitress. She put the money in the center console of the car.

There was now a small crowd outside the bar: me, Pavel, the four assholes, Scorpio and his two friends and another six bystanders.

"You beat me and the money is yours," I told the irate asshole. He sneered then lunged at me. I grabbed his forearm and hip-tossed him on to the ground, keeping hold of his arm. I rolled him onto his stomach, twisted his arm and drove my knee between his shoulder blades. His friends just looked on. Scorpio and his friends didn't need to do anything. They stood there watching with beers in hands.

"Tonight's the last time you shoot pool for money," I told the asshole pinned under me. "Don't come around here. If you see me or any of my friends again, just mind your own business. You understand me?"

"Yeah, yeah. Ok. I'm done," he said with a mouthful of gravel. I got off his back as the bar manager came outside.

Before the manager could say anything, Pavel said, "It's all over, Paddy. Nobody is hurt."

The manager said since everyone was outside and it was an hour to closing, we should all leave. My girlfriend had watched the outdoor exchange from her car with Joe passed out in the front seat. I made a driving motion with my hands and waved her to go. She drove off.

"Let's go," Pavel said. We got into his car and drove to my girlfriend's house.

"I got to learn those moves," Pavel said while driving. "That Tae Kwon Do is amazing shit."

"Kicking the beer out their hands was the only Tae Kwon Do thing I did. It's called a hook kick. Probably the least powerful kick there is, but effective when you surprise them," I replied. "The throw-down was jiu-jitsu."

At my girlfriend's house, Joe was awake recalling the events of the evening with a shot of vodka and a cigarette which in itself was a sign of his inebriation because he didn't smoke. My girlfriend counted over $1500 from Joe's winning. Joe insisted I take the money since I saved his life. In the end we split the money four ways.

My girlfriend noticed it was 3AM and declared it was time for everyone to go to sleep. Pavel was already passed out on the sofa. I poured Joe into a bed in the spare room. He insisted I set an alarm for 7AM. He was meeting a friend for a round of golf at 8AM. He wasn't going anywhere for a while I thought as I crawled into bed next to my girlfriend.

I awoke around 8:30 that morning. Pavel was still passed out on the sofa. I started the coffee machine and noticed a note on the counter.

Thanks for a great night. Joe

College Big Brother I

Throughout my life I believe that I have experienced times of "fast-tracked maturity." I discovered certain responsibilities were thrown at me that I did not want but I dealt with the scenario. During that process, I developed skills for coaching, mentoring or just being a better person in general. My last year in college was what I describe as my "big brother" year. I became the big brother to all the underclassmen at the college, especially those that lived on-campus.

I worked during my college years; my parents did not contribute financially to my college education. I paid for the tuition and living expenses through student loans and part-time work as a bouncer or bartender at the bars at LaClede's Landing along the St. Louis riverfront. I also worked during the week as a Laboratory teaching assistant at the college. All the part-time work adversely affected my grades, so I had to "overload" my final two semesters. "Overload" meant exceeding the maximum 18 hours class-time per week for a full-time student. I was also teaching Math and Physics classes to the non-Engineering students because the professor assigned to those classes thought it was beneath his status to directly teach the students. I had nearly as many hours teaching per week as I did as a student.

Working for the college provided more exposure to underclassman. I was already well-known on campus for being the tallest person at the college. Students that missed a class or a laboratory would ask me for a make-up session. Certain classes would allow a single make-up session for a missed class or lab. I would have informal, unofficial make-up sessions for beer, pizza or laundry money. The weekends that I hoped would be used for my studying and projects turned into an extension of my teaching job. I also found myself being a marriage counsellor to some of the married students or a mentor to others.

My second to last semester was a summer semester and I was back in the Mercury Hall dormitory. For the previous year and a half, I lived in the apartment complex across the street from the college, but my roommate moved out to live with his girlfriend and I could no longer afford the apartment on my own. Students were offered only 50% the normal room and board rate to live in Mercury Hall during the summer semester because the 40 year old air conditioning system was being replaced - probably because it was rumored there was a case of Legionnaire's disease in the dorm the previous semester. The summer was a brutally hot and humid one for the St. Louis area that year. The heat started early and didn't let up until late autumn.

I was living on the first floor of Mercury Hall. There was a junior year student named Steve that also lived on the first floor who was not to be denied the comforts he desired. He had a 34 inch color television and a VCR in his dorm room. He also had a mini-refrigerator and a window unit air conditioner. These items seem like no big deal today, but back in the mid-1980's, Steve was living like a king for a student!

One Friday night, Steve and a few other underclassmen were watching movies in his dorm room. I wandered over to Steve's room close to midnight – I had been working on one of my senior design projects throughout the evening and I decided to join them for a beer and watch part of a movie. I assumed they would be watching a science fiction movie or some stupid 80's comedy. I entered the room to see on the television a monkey being brained by diners using small wooden hammers in a restaurant. They were watching "Faces of Death".

91

"Faces of Death" was a cult horror film from the late 1970's. The movie consisted of unedited footage of animals and humans being killed. I recall seeing the monkey scene and a man attacked, then eaten by an alligator, and an execution by electric chair. It was a gruesome film. The men in the room made comments and squirmed while watching the film. One kid, Paulie, said he saw enough and left. About ten minutes later, we heard a commotion in the hallway. Someone was banging on the doors yelling for help.

"There's a guy bleeding on the stairs! I think he's dead! Someone call an ambulance!" yelled a kid I didn't recognize.

"What's going on?" I asked as we emptied Steve's room.

"That kid Paulie is bleeding on the stairs," he yelled, pointing to the north stairway.

"Go find an RA or a security guard. Tell them what's going on," I told one of the movie viewers. "Take me to Paulie."

We ran to the stairway to find Paulie laying on the stairs, facedown with his head turned slightly. There was blood on his face and on the floor below his head. He was covered in sweat as we all were due to the unventilated building, but Paulie was thoroughly soaked.

I braced the back of his neck with my left hand and gently shook his shoulder with my right hand, "Paulie, are you awake?"

He was breathing, I saw bubbles in the corner of his mouth made from drool and sweat. He moaned.

"Guys let's move him up a few stairs onto the mid-level area," I told the group. I secured Paulie's head at the base of his neck while the others, one on each limb, lifted Paulie a few inches above the stairs and moved him to the mid-level section of the stairway. It was a difficult task - his arms were slick with sweat, as were the kids' hands that were moving him. We placed Paulie on his back with his head facing up. His forehead was split open from just below the hairline to the top of his right eyebrow. The bleeding lessened with his head in the face-up position. The split was wide enough to see his skull.

"Somebody go find a first aid kit. Steve, get some wet towels. Put ice in one of them," I said.

When the first aid kit and towels appeared, I told Steve to press the cool wet towels against Paulie's cheeks to cool him down. I used another towel and gauze from the first aid kit to clean his forehead. Paulie flickered his eyes and groaned.

"Paulie, what happened?" I asked as I carefully wiped his forehead.

"I was going to my room," Paulie whispered, "I wasn't feeling good. I got dizzy."

"You busted your head open. Don't move. How are you feeling now?"

"I don't know."

"Are you going to throw up?"

"No, I don't think so."

"Stay still. You going to need to have this wound stitched together. We called an ambulance."

The kid that went to get the security guard returned. He couldn't find the guard and the security office was locked. He couldn't find the RA either. I told him the guard was probably making his rounds.

"Go find a RA in the other dorm," I told him. "If you still can't find one, go to the Housing Director's apartment. Tell her about Paulie. Call 911 if you have to."

The group was whispering among themselves for a while but now started asking Paulie questions. I told them to stop crowding too close. Give him room to breathe.

Steve continued to press wet towels to Paulie's cheeks. I continued to gently clean his forehead and apply ice as best I could without pressing on the gash. Several minutes went by and Paulie was feeling uncomfortable. He had been lying in the same position for a while. He was getting fidgety. Then I noticed that gash was getting longer. It grew slightly toward his hairline, but the end of the gash originally near the eyebrow had creeped into the eyebrow. Paulie was overweight and his face was pudgy. The weight of his face was opening the gash. As it grew longer, it also grew wider. I could see more of his skull through the opening.

"Are there any butterfly strips in the first aid kit?" I asked. One of the guys searched through the kit. He found a small packet containing the strips. The contents were yellowed with age.

"Hey Paulie, I'm going to tape the wound together, OK? I think it's a good idea to close this so sweat doesn't get in the cut. Try not to move."

"Ok," Paulie replied. He shuddered slightly.

I pinched the gash together and applied two butterfly strips. The adhesive on the strips was old and combined with his moist forehead, the butterfly closure failed. I told Dave to retrieve a roll of athletic tape from my closet. When Dave returned, I tore off a long strip of the white, zinc-coated tape. I pinched the wound closed again and taped his entire forehead. It looked like it finally held.

The security guard arrived. He quizzed everyone about what happened for his night report. Paulie wanted to sit up, but I told him he had to stay down until paramedics cleared him to get up. It seemed to me the situation was under control. The tape covered most of the gash. The ends of it were slightly uncovered. Blood welled in the tiny gaps. I was about to soak up the blood with a tissue when I saw Paulie's forehead move under the tape. It wasn't holding. He was sweating too much. In a split second, the tape gave way and the gash spread through his eyebrow.

I squeezed Paulie's forehead together and removed the tape. I did my best not to say anything, but I shook my head and frowned. Paulie noticed and became scared again.

"Guys, are there any sutures in the first aid kit?" I asked. The atmosphere became heavy as the group realized the situation just got worse. There were no sutures in the kit. Everyone started offering ideas of finding a sewing kit for needle and thread or using a stapler. The security guard suggested looking in the medical office in the other dorm, Holloran Hall. A doctor from the main campus visited every Tuesday and he used a small office on the first floor of the A-block of Holloran Hall for seeing students. Perhaps there was something in there? The guard had keys to the office. He took two boys with him. They returned with a suture kit, alcohol and two girls (the A-block of Holloran Hall was the girl's dormitory). One of the girls prepped the suture needle and soaked the thread in alcohol.

"Paulie, the cut is getting longer. One end is really close to your eye. Tape isn't working. I think sewing it is the only way to stop the cut from getting to your eye. Are you ok if I do this?"

"Uh-huh. Do it."

I remember being surprised and relieved that Paulie never asked me if I had sewn a wound before. I never did. This was completely new to me. I didn't want the gash to get to his eyelid. I didn't know if it would split open like the forehead did, and I didn't want to find out. Paulie was scared and I didn't want him to panic more by thinking I didn't know what I was doing. And I didn't want to growing crowd of people thinking the same thing.

"Keep your eyes closed Paulie. When I poke you, it might sting. Don't move. Stay relaxed," I said, "Did I ever tell you about the time I heard a drunk student's confession in the men's room just down the hall?"

I started telling the story as I stuck the suture needle into Paulie's forehead. I got as close to the eyelid as I dared. I pushed the curved needle as deep as it would go before bringing it up on the other side of the gash. I closed the gap with the first stitch, moving onto the second stitch, telling my story to Paulie and the crowd. Luckily the ice and wet towels had numbed his forehead enough for Paulie to not feel the poking and tugging of the sutures; and the story seemed to calm him, too.

As I attempted another stitch, someone noticed red flashing lights through a window. The security guard said he would get the paramedics and left the stairway. I continued with the sewing. It wasn't pretty. I was sewing as if I was repairing a hole in a sock. There were uneven gaps between stitches and the hook holes on either side of the gash were asymmetrical. The paramedics finally came in, appraising the situation, asking questions. I asked the nearest paramedic if he wanted to take over for me. He hooked the final two stitches in a few seconds (compared to my one-stitch-a-minute ability). The two paramedics lifted Paulie onto a gurney. The crowd clapped and whistled as they rolled Paulie toward the ambulance. The paramedic that finished the stitching told me I made a good decision to stop the cut from spreading.

I saw Paulie the next day with a bandage taped across his forehead. He talked about the rest of the night he spent in the Firmin-Desloge hospital at the St. Louis University main campus. Emergency room nurses cleaned his wound. A plastic surgeon was called in to undo my stitch work and close the wound properly.

A few days later, I was leaving a classroom when I was intercepted by Dr. Whelan, the dean of Parks College. Dr. Whelan thanked me for taking charge of a student emergency over the weekend. He mentioned the briefing he received from the Director of Housing and the phone call from Paulie's parents. All this praise was said in front of my friends. I received pats on the back and razzes about how I should change my studies from engineering to medicine. During the graduation ceremony held at the end of the summer semester, I was invited to attend the event where I was presented with a letter and certificate of appreciation from the Deans of the University for my actions that hot and humid night.

Dennis Hannaway

Epilogue: Two years later, I was working at Douglas Aircraft Company in Long Beach, California. I saw Paulie, walking through the parking lot after work one afternoon. We hadn't seen each other for a while, so we went to a bar near work. Over a few rounds of beer, we reminisced about that night, and we were able to laugh about it.

College Big Brother II

During my last two semesters, I was back in the dorms. My final semester was in Holloran Hall, specifically the B-block. The room next to me was occupied by identical twins: Andy and Randy Trucks. Andy and Randy were sophomores in the Aircraft Maintenance Management program. I taught their Basic Physics class when they were freshmen.

Three weeks into the semester, there was a big party off-campus hosted by one of the fraternities. I avoided events like that during my last semester. Me and my fellow graduating seniors, Oscar and Jay, enjoyed a few pitchers of beer at STOOGES, the bar next to campus, on that Friday night. We walked back to our dorm rooms before midnight. I had been in bed for about an hour when I was rudely awoken by a phone that wouldn't stop ringing in Andy's and Randy's room. It was their fraternity that was having the party, so I knew they weren't going to be back for a few hours. Why didn't whoever was calling them know that too? The phone rang incessantly for more than ten minutes, and I couldn't take it anymore. I carded my way into their dorm room to answer the phone.

"Hello!" I said angrily into the phone. I was going to say a lot more, but I was cut off Andy's panicky voice on the line.

"Dennis! Me and Randy are in the Cahokia jail. Can you bail us out?"

"What'd you do?" I asked.

"The cops arrested us for underage drinking."

"Were you driving?"

"No, they broke up the party. A cop asked for my ID. I gave it to him, but I was f'd up."

"Well, that's good. Just spend the night in the jail cell and they will release you in the morning."

"No, they say that we have to be bailed out. Our parents will kill us if they get a call tomorrow."

I had maybe twenty dollars in my possession. Andy said there was forty dollars in their room. He didn't know how much their bail was. I asked Andy to give the phone to the desk officer so I could talk to him.

"Yea?" said the voice on the phone.

"Hi, he asked me to bail out him and his brother. How much is it?" I asked.

"Are you his father?" the officer replied.

"No."

"Then this call is over." Click. Great, I thought. They must have mouthed off while getting arrested and pissed off the entire staff of three officers on night shift. I found their car keys on a desk, then drove to the police station.

The police station was in the Village Hall building. It had two holding cells. Occupants in the holding cells didn't stay long; they were either bailed out or taken to the county facility near Belleville. I arrived to see a police officer sitting at a desk drinking a Coke, reading a magazine.

"What can I do for you?" the officer asked.

"I'm the one they called to get them out," I replied.

He laughed, "That's two hundred dollars."

"Fifty is the best I can do."

"Nope. That won't work."

"Is there no room to negotiate? Fifty is all I got."

"After the way those two mouthed off, I don't think so."

Now I was stuck. Thoughts of going back to the dorms and waking people to come up with the money were running through my mind. That was something I did not want to do. As I was pondering this conundrum, I noticed how unkempt the office was. The walls were dirty and could use fresh paint. I imagined the restrooms were probably a mess. Then an idea popped in my mind.

"Sorry to hear that those knuckleheads mouthed off. This has been a waste of my time. I'm sorry to have wasted yours." I said apologetically to the officer. "Can I tell them they will have to talk to their parents? I really want to see the look of panic on their faces since they got my ass out of bed for nothing."

The officer escorted me through the room to the cell where the twins were sitting on a bench. They look excited as I approached the cell.

"Sorry boys. I don't have enough money to get you out. You all failed your folks, and you failed me."

They had a quizzical look on their faces.

"Dude, what do ya mean?" Randy asked.

"Yeah, dude. What's going on?" Andy chimed in.

"I've tried to be a big brother to you guys. Give you a good example..." They looked flabbergasted. I could tell they were thinking 'what is he talking about?'

"Mouthing off to the officers was a dumbass move. No way to get you out." I turned to walk out. I gave the officer a look of futility. Then looked around. "It's too bad you can't have those boys put a fresh coat of paint in here," I said.

"Yeah, it could use it," the officer replied.

"Rather than go through the hassle of processing these two, how about getting a day's work out of them?" I suggested. "They could wash the walls, fresh coat of paint, clean the restrooms, wash the cars...those boys are mechanics, they can tune up the patrol cars. It would teach them a lesson for mouthing off."

"It's a good idea, but that has to be negotiated," he replied.

"Let's negotiate. Let them sleep in the cell tonight. I'll be back around seven. I'll order them around so you aren't put into a conflict of interest situation, but drop the charges against them."

He thought about it for a minute. I could tell by his facial expression that he liked the idea.

"Alright," he said, "I'll have a list ready in the morning. I'll let the next shift know what's going on."

"Thanks, let me tell those knuckleheads I'll be back in the morning."

I told the boys that if they slept in jail tonight, I might get them out in the morning without charges being filed. They asked for details, but I wanted them surprised in the morning. I hoped they would be more cooperative that way.

I returned to the dorm for a few hours of sleep. I got up before seven, went to the dining hall where I was immediately chastised for entering before the 10:30 opening time. I explained I needed sandwiches and coffee for the boys in jail, telling the kitchen captain the whole story. She was amused and bagged cereal, milk, bread, bowls, spoons and coffee for me. I arrived at the police station shortly after seven. The three evening officers had already left and the three weekend day shift officers were there. The lead officer presented a long list of chores that included cleaning the toilets, washing windows, landscaping and other tasks that would be unappealing while nursing a hangover. He opened their cell. I nudged the twins awake with my foot. The three officers watched as I handed the breakfast to the groggy twins.

"This is from Maggie in the Dining Hall, you need to thank her tomorrow," I started. "So, here's the deal. Here is a list of chores you boys need to accomplish today. I worked it out with the officers last night that if you complete this list of chores today, they may not process you. That means you would be free to go without this incident on your record and your folks will never know. I have to be here to supervise. When you finish a chore and I find it acceptable, I'll have one of the officers inspect it and they have to approve too. Otherwise, you keep doing it."

Andy and Randy grumbled their acceptance of the terms. They dragged ass out of the cell after they finished their breakfast.

"Andy, start scrubbing the walls in the hallway and in the cells," I said.

"There's a bucket and Pine Sol in the closet," an officer pointed. Randy snickered at his brother.

"Randy, looks like you have shithole duty," I told him.

"Aw dude, did you see those toilets? Aw, come on," Randy complained.

"Do I have to call your mom?" I asked.

"Okay, okay," he said. The officers laughed. When they both seemed to be progressing on their first task, I took a book out of my bag to work on a class project. I made sure they kept working while I worked on calculations. Randy claimed he was done with the toilets in less than fifteen minutes. I took a look at his job and told him to scrub each toilet again inside and out; and clean the sinks and wash the walls and floors. Randy was not pleased. Andy laughed and I pointed out every little flaw in the job he was doing.

"Don't forget, the gentlemen in uniform have the final say as to whether it's done, so stop trying to short cut your way out of this mess."

Both moaned and got back to it. They began to entertain themselves as they worked. They sang "Midnight Special" and "Cotton Fields" while they labored away, drawing laughs from the officers. Occasionally we would all sing along with the boys. Both finished their initial chore. The officer performed a white glove inspection while the boys watched. The officer nodded his approval. Next came painting the walls that were just washed, then cleaning the windows – interior and exterior. Andy's and Randy's hard work and occasional antics rubbed off on the policeman in the office. He began to empty trash cans, organize stacks of files and other busy work. Four hours later, the station looked super clean and organized. The officer's wife arrived with his lunch and sandwiches for me and the twins – apparently, he called home earlier to ask his wife to bring extra. The small breakfast the boys had earlier only postponed their hangover hunger for an hour or two. The sandwiches were enjoyed while they took a short break. The lady commented on how good the office looked. She had never seen it so clean.

The afternoon was full of outdoor chores: cleaning gutters, picking weeds and trimming bushes. An officer gave me a folding table and chair to set up in a shady spot while I continued my overseer duties and worked on my projects. The officers were impressed with the boys. Andy and Randy were their normal respectful selves while they worked. The officers appreciated their efforts and the inspections passed much easier.

The final chore on the list was to wash the cars at the maintenance garage. The officer that provided lunch had the boys get into the back seat of the patrol car for the ride to the garage. I got into the front seat. As the car entered the street, it hesitated momentarily then moved along. It seemed there was a lack of power.

"The plugs are fowled," Randy said.

"Or maybe the cables have gone bad," Andy chimed.

"Yeah maybe," Randy agreed.

The officer slowed down for a stop light. The brakes whined as the car pulled to the left.

"Pads are shot," Randy offered.

"Got to turn the rotors," Andy suggested.

We arrived at the maintenance garage. The officer let them out of the back of the car. Randy told the officer to open the hood and turn on the car. Andy walked into the garage and returned with a tarp. I threw the tarp over the open hood to block the sunlight as the four of us looked at the engine. Half of the spark plug cables had flashing lights appearing from inside the cables. I popped the distributor cap off the rotor. The metal caps were tarnished.

"You need new plugs, cables and a distributor cap," I told the officer. We made a list of items to get from the auto parts store. The officer went to buy the parts while we jacked the front end and removed the wheels. The brake pads were shot. The boys bled the brakes. The officer returned with all we needed to repair the brakes and distributor systems. Andy and Randy worked on brake rotor and calipers while I dealt with changing the spark plugs, cables and distributor cap – now I was pulled into doing chores!

When we were done working on the car and lowered it from the jack, the officer took it for a test drive. He mentioned the brakes were jerky. Randy said that he would need to drive the car before taking the wheels off again. The officer opened the door, "Be my guest."

Randy got into the driver's side, Andy on the passenger side. They took it for a drive around the block. They came back saying there must have been air in the brake line and it purged itself during their test drive. The jerkiness was gone. I told them to pop the hood. I opened the master cylinder seeing the fluid level was lower than before. I agreed with their conclusion. Randy asked the officer if he wanted to drive it again. The officer got into the back seat. They enjoyed driving a police cruiser, especially with an officer in the back. The only thing missing from that experience was that they didn't have the blue spinning lights and siren on.

When they returned to the garage, the boys washed the car as their final chore. And in true Andy and Randy form, they started a water fight. I was doused with a bucket of dirty water. I wrestled the hose from them and soaked them. The police crew was pleased with all the work that was completed. They brought us ice cream cones. The record of the arrest was 'lost.' Andy and Randy were free to go.

Word spread around campus about the deal that was struck for Andy and Randy. I received compliments from students, instructors and custodial staff alike throughout the week. That Friday at STOOGES, I was with Jay and Oscar enjoying pitchers of beer paid for by students while we tossed horseshoes in the evening. I walked back to the dorm and had just laid down when Andy's and Randy's phone rang and wouldn't stop. I entered their room and answered the phone.

"Hello, is this Dennis? This is Officer Williams from the Cahokia Police Department. Do you know a student named Monty?"

Dog Adoption I

I am a dog lover. I've had dogs all my life. There were brief periods when I was without a dog, usually no more than three years. My father raised English Pointers. He enjoyed the sport of field trialing. He wasn't good at it, but he enjoyed it.

Field trialing is a competition of dog and handler teams in a simulated game-bird hunting scenario. The dog is judged on its ability to find birds, point to the location of the bird and hold its "point" until released by its handler. The handler is also judged on his or her ability to communicate with the dog and work together as a team.

I also participated in field trialing. I won a handful of competitions. I spent my youth training and maintaining our hunting dogs. When I graduated from college and moved to California to start my Aerospace career, it was the first time I was ever without a dog in my life.

My first dog after I began my Aerospace career was a golden retriever named Sally. She was an inaugural Father's Day gift from my wife and step kids. My wife found Sally in a Petland store in the Lakewood Mall. Sally was four months old and crammed into a small dog-sized cage barely able to move. Sally was a great dog and loved kids. She would sleep with the kids. They would lay on her. If she

106

wasn't playing with them, she would stand watch over their play area and get between the kids and any stranger that approached. About a week after receiving Sally, we drove to my mother's house for a visit. My mother had a swimming pool, and the kids were always wanting to go to "Garma's" to have fun in the water. Being a retriever, Sally was a natural swimmer. She and the kids had a ball in the pool. My step-daughter Sarah, who was 22 months old at the time, was repeatedly trying to sneak into the pool without adult supervision. She finally got away with it. She fell into the pool with a splash. I bolted out of my chair and ran through a screen door to rescue her, but Sally beat me to it. Sally jumped into the pool and immediately swam to Sarah and brought her head above water. Sarah grabbed Sally's tail as the dog paddled to the pool stairs. Impressive for a four month old puppy!

Four years after Sally arrived, we were living in Lancaster, CA. I had been working for a defense contractor at the Edwards Air Force Base, but in1993 I transferred from a military program to a commercial aircraft program. I had to commute to a facility in Long Beach – a 100 mile drive from driveway to parking lot. I would spend Monday and Tuesday night in Long Beach, staying at a friend's house, then drive home Wednesday night. Thursday morning I drove to Long Beach, spent the night there, then I'd drive home Friday afternoon. My wife was not happy with her and the kids being alone in the house three nights a week. Sally was a comfort, but she still felt vulnerable. Around the time I started the commute, Sally had an epileptic seizure. She was on phenobarbital ever since. Her reactions/responses seemed slightly slower than normal, but overall she was fine. After doing the commute for a year, my wife told me she wanted another dog. If Sally had to defend the family, she would need help. I thought Sally was formidable enough, despite the phenobarbital. At four years old, Sally was a large Golden Retriever. She stood 28 inches to her shoulder and weighed 80 pounds. She had a deep voice, so her growl and bark would easily frighten an intruder. My wife was adamant, and Sally would benefit with having a companion. I said that if a guard dog was what she wanted, then we should look into getting a Rottweiler.

I came home from work on a Friday night and there was a six week old Rottweiler puppy sleeping on a cushion in the living room. The wife and kids named her Samantha or Sammy for short. Sally overcame a 30 minute period of dejection and sadness, then took to her new companion with great fondness. Sammy also loved kids. They would squeeze her paws or tug her docked tail, that they called her 'nubby', all things that Rottweilers usually do not tolerate, but Sammy only allowed the kids to do it.

Sally and Sammy were our canine family for the next two and a half years. Sally passed away in 1996 from an intestinal infection. A veterinarian diagnosed Sally with having a uterine infection and recommended she be spade. Either she had the infection when the vet did the procedure and he failed to see the condition when her belly was open, or he damaged the intestine during the surgery. Unfortunately, Sally endured four days of pain before she died.

Sammy went through a three week period of lonesomeness as we all did after Sally's loss. There was never competition between Sally and Sammy for affection, but with Sally gone, Sammy was the recipient of all the love and affection – the three cats were probably annoyed. Two years later, my wife appeared with another dog that she named Ginger. This dog was a pointer/chocolate lab mix, approximately two years old. I cannot recall how she found Ginger. I believed Ginger was abused by a previous owner. She never barked. She was also a notorious digger. She dug holes under the house and shrubs in order to hide. I was never able to form a bond with Ginger.

About a year or so later, my wife and I divorced. She took Sammy; and I was without a dog for nearly two years. In 2001, I was really missing having a dog. The local NBC television affiliate produced a public service advertisement for the local Humane Society called "Pet

Playhouse." The Playhouse was a 90 second segment that featured a cat or dog for adoption. For three consecutive days Pet Playhouse featured an adult female Rottweiler named Elizabeth. She was a beautiful dog that reminded me of Sammy. Since the ad ran for three days, I concluded Elizabeth had not been adopted; so maybe I should visit the Humane Society and meet the dog.

I went to the Humane Society after work. I was greeted by a girl at the main entrance. She asked how she could help me. I mentioned seeing a Rottweiler named Elizabeth on Pet Playhouse and I would like to meet her. The girl told me that Elizabeth had mammary cancer and was put down earlier that day. I said I was sorry to hear that. She asked if I was interested in a different dog, but I said no and wanted to leave. She suggested that I look around anyway, so I did. I walked into the kennel area. The nearest were the small dog kennels. There were many cute small and toy sized dogs of all ages. I remember that I had played with a rambunctious Boston Terrier for a while. I also visited a litter of Beagle puppies. As I passed each kennel, I tried to give each dog a minute or two of attention. I slowly made my way into the larger dog section. There were a lot of shepherd mix and retriever mix dogs. Lots of mutts. I walked down the final aisle of kennels, and as I turned a corner, I saw two Rottweilers sharing a large kennel. They looked to be under a year old. A paper on the kennel door showed:

Name: Duke
Name: Daisy
Breed: Rottweiler
Age: about 10 months old, littermates, always been together

Daisy was a good-sized female, smaller than I remembered Sammy at 10 months, with "American" Rottweiler features. Her tail was docked at the base vertebrae. She had a sweet demeanor. Duke was a large male and by the looks of his paws, he was going to be a lot bigger. He had classic "German" Rottweiler features with a wide head. He would cross his eyes if something was close to his nose. When I got on my knees to get a close look at him, he leaned against me, trying to force me to sit down. He wanted to sit on my lap! I loved on both dogs for a long time. My last two dogs were females, so I was contemplating whether I should adopt Daisy. She was very attentive and didn't show any signs of mischief. Since they have always been together, I was concerned that either dog could have separation anxiety if I adopted only Daisy. I lived by myself and I believed I could handle one dog. Two dogs would have been too much for me. I decided I could not separate them, so I gave each dog a final hug. They watched me with their ears perked up as I walked away toward the exit. The same girl that greeted me caught me before I made it out the building. She asked if I saw any dog that interested me. I mentioned the Rottweilers and that I considered adopting the female, but I couldn't bring myself to separating them. The girl asked if she could get my information for future arrivals – maybe a dog will arrive that I would like. She excused herself to get the necessary form.

I looked around the office. There was a large whiteboard on the wall. There were names of animals on the whiteboard along with their kennel location and a date next to each name. Daisy and Duke were on the top of the list with tomorrow's date. The girl returned with a form for me to complete. I asked what the list of names on the whiteboard were for. She replied that it was the euthanize dates for the animals that were at the shelter too long.

"I'll adopt the Rottweilers!" I said.

I signed the adoption papers. According to state law, rescue animals required neutering before the animal could be received by the new owner. The staff at the Humane Shelter scheduled the procedures with the veterinarian of my choice on the following business day, Monday. My Rotties had to stay at the shelter for two more days.

I spent the weekend getting food, bowls for food and water and a pooper-scooper. I also went to the shelter both days for an hour each day to spend time with the dogs. I wanted them to get used to me being around. I quickly discovered that they did not know how to play. All their life, they were lucky to get 30 minutes a day outside of a cage or a small kennel run. They had no interest in a ball or a tug-of-war toy. They just stood around looking at me wondering what to do. I did get them to chase me at times. Chasing was something I didn't want them to do, but I wanted some kind of positive interfacing with them.

I was finally allowed to take possession of the dogs at the vet's office after they had a brief recovery period from the surgeries. The vet said the dogs were to remain inactive for three to four more days, so I didn't let them jump in and out of the truck; I loaded and unloaded each dog myself. They explored their new home for a while, always looking back at me when they entered a different room. I guided them into the back yard. It was just under a quarter acre in area with a seven foot tall privacy fence and a swimming pool. I monitored their exploration of the yard. They cautioned the pool very well. I was confident that when their mandatory inactivity period was over, they would be fine to be unsupervised in the yard.

I decided it was time to tell my girlfriend that I adopted the dogs. We were in a long distance relationship and when we talked over the weekend, I didn't mention anything. We had been dating for nearly a year. Should I have included her on a decision like this? She had a dog. Would she be ok with two more dogs in this relationship? I guess I had not said anything because I didn't have them yet. The breakfast nook in the kitchen area had large windows so I could easily watch the dogs while they stayed in the yard.

As I thought, she was not thrilled at first to learn that I adopted two dogs and Rottweilers at that. We had been talking for ten minutes when Duke ran to the kitchen window barking. I looked for Daisy but couldn't see her. I looked to the far side of the pool and saw Daisy splashing in the water. She fell into the pool! I ran outside to rescue her. She was swimming as best she could. I went to the pool stairs to coax her out of the water. I nearly jumped in but realized now was the time to teach her how to use the pool stairs. She paddled furiously, eventually making it up the stairs. I checked her incision hoping she did not tear the sutures. She looked ok and I brought her into the laundry room.

I dried her with an oversized towel. I knew I had to keep a close watch on her for the next few hours to check for signs of internal bleeding. As I dried her, I could swear she smiled. She licked my face as I toweled her head. She stood still while I worked. I felt terrible that she fell in the pool. Duke came to me wanting attention like his sister was getting. As I worked on Daisy, I released that I really disliked their names. I looked at her as I finished drying her and her name came to me.

"You're a Morgan,' I said to her. She stepped into my lap and licked my face.

My female Rottweiler was now named Morgan. She took to her name immediately. Now for Duke - what to call him? Many names went through my head, but nothing seemed appealing. I entertained 'Max' for a few minutes, but it didn't seem right. What name would go well with a sibling named Morgan? I almost thought about changing her name to help me think of a good one for him when it dawned on me. Morgan le Fay. Arthurian legend. Morgan le Fay's brother was King Arthur! I'll call him Arthur. But that didn't seem right either. Then I remembered reading a book called "Firelord" by Parke Godwin. In it, Arthur was frequently called 'Artos', a Welch diminutive of the name Arthur. Artos, that fit! My Rottweilers were Artos and Morgan.

Need to Pay Better Attention...

Sometimes the most benign test flight can become the most risky event an organization can face. As a Flight Test Engineer (FTE), I flew hundreds, perhaps thousands, of hours on flights with no more risk than an ordinary commercial airline flight; and I also flew on the most dangerous tests required to certify an airframe.

In the early 2000s I was the Chief FTE for the GIV-X program, and I was also the lead FTE for Aero-performance, Flying Qualities, Mechanical Systems and Propulsion disciplines in the Flight Test Engineering organization. My coworker, Walt Astill, was the Chief FTE for the GV-SP program and he also doubled as the lead FTE Avionics, Autopilot and Electrical Systems disciplines. Another coworker, Karl Broenner, was the Chief FTE for the entire organization.

One day, Karl asked me to prepare an engine pylon ventilation test on the GV-SP test aircraft, S/N 632. It was a repeat of a test that was completed a few weeks earlier. For whatever reason that I cannot recall, the test needed to be repeated and it was also a certification test. Karl was the FAA Designated Engineering Representative (DER) for this specific test. He was responsible to witness the test and the recording of the data as the DER; he could not conduct the test, so he asked me to do it. As I prepared the flight cards, Walt said he wanted to add a few Enhanced Vision System (EVS) tests to the deck as tag-along non-certification tests. EVS was one of Walt's projects and he was always looking for an opportunity to get more data for the system. Walt recommended I have the Chief Test Pilot, Ian McGlenich, fly the test. Ian was the project pilot for EVS and he was one of the DER pilots approved for the pylon ventilation test.

The day of the test fell on a Friday. It was also one of the busiest days on the flight schedule. Nearly all the test pilots were on the flight schedule that day. Karl, Walt and I arrived in the Flight Operations briefing room for the preflight meeting. Andy Serf, the Vice President of Flight Operations, called out to us, "Mister Dennis, Mister Walt, Mister Karl, what brings you three here?"

"Pylon ventilation test," I replied, "and Walt wants to do a few EVS tests, too."

"Who are your pilots?" Andy asked.

"Ian, but the other pilot isn't assigned yet. Karl is looking for a volunteer."

"I'll go," Andy said.

We briefed the test and off we went. The flight manifest was:

> Pilot-in-Command: Ian (DER)
> Pilot: Andy as copilot
> Test Conductor: Dennis
> Test Engineer: Walt
> Test Engineer: Karl (DER)

The pylon ventilation test was uneventful. Karl monitored the data at a workstation in the back of the airplane. The test passed and he was satisfied with the results. Walt was watching the EVS display on a repeater screen at another workstation. I was in the cockpit with the pilots going over the completed test cards before we moved on to the approaches Walt wanted to do for the EVS. Then we were hailed on the company Flight Test radio frequency.

"FT two zero, Flight Test," the voice said over the VHF.

"Flight Test, FT two zero, go ahead," I replied.

"Two zero, you are to RTB."

"Flight Test, we estimate RTB in one hour."

"Negative on the one hour, two zero. RTB now."

"Please explain Flight Test. I have good air and things to do."

"Don't argue with me Dennis," a different voice said over the frequency. It was Ben, the Director of Flight Test.

"What's the problem, Ben?" Ian said, taking over comms.

"You have an unapproved manifest," Ben replied.

"What is he talking about?" Andy asked us over the internal com.

I looked at the manifest listed on the cover page of the test cards. Then it dawned on me as I viewed it from a different perspective:

> Pilot-in-Command: Chief Test Pilot
>
> Pilot: Vice President, Flight Operations
>
> Test Conductor: Chief Flight Test Engineer, GIV-X
>
> Test Engineer: Chief Flight Test Engineer, GV-SP
>
> Test Engineer: Chief Flight Test Engineer

Before I could tell Andy, Ben chimed in again, "All of Flight Test and Flight Ops leadership on one flight is unacceptable. RTB at once!"

"How'd we let that happen?" Andy asked. Then we all laughed.

"I really want to do these approaches before we go," Ian said, and Walt concurred.

"Let's head to Cartersville and do these approaches," Walt said.

"Yeah, well I'm getting hungry," Karl said.

"After the approaches, let's land in Cartersville and have lunch? There're a few mall food places near the FBO," Ian said.

"That will make them wet their pants," Andy smiled.

"Flight Test, FT two zero," Ian said over the frequency, "we're going to do an approach card then RTB."

"Roger that, two zero. See you soon. Flight Test out."

Andy and Ian flew at least six approaches into the Cartersville Regional Airport. We landed after the final approach. The FBO attendant drove us to an AppleBees restaurant where we had lunch, taking our time and savoring the knowledge that Ben and a few others were wondering why we hadn't returned.

We returned to base about two and half hours after we said we were heading home. As we held our post-flight briefing, we were joined by Ben and the Senior Vice President for Engineering, Programs and Test. We received a lecture about how we endangered the company by placing all the Flight leadership assets on one test vehicle. An accident would have wiped out too many irreplaceable employees. New rules were made to ensure no more than two leaders were on the same flight for future operations.

At the Supermarket III

Did you ever avoid going to a store because of an embarrassing event that you witnessed? Not necessarily that you were the subject of the embarrassment, but perhaps a person that tried to drag you and others into it? When I lived in Richmond Hill, Georgia, the closest grocery store was a Publix supermarket only five miles away, but I would drive ten miles to Kroger or Food Lion because there was a crazy woman who always shopped at Publix.

The woman in question had nine kids. She had personality issues with a reputation to explode into screaming episodes, especially to people she knew. Even her husband told everyone that she was crazy. Unfortunately, I was in the store when I witnessed one such event.

This woman was shopping with the seven youngest children of the brood. During the foray, what started as a single shopping cart of groceries became a train of many carts full of junk food, soda, and beer. As the carts filled up, the woman and her kids became louder and ruder as they roamed the aisles. When their shopping was done, the woman lined up the train of carts at a closed checkout station and demanded the store get a cashier over to her immediately. To any store patron she saw, she would yell, "It's all on EBT! I'm not paying a cent for this! You are! It's on EBT!"

Eventually, the woman left her husband and moved out of state with the kids. Needless to say, the neighborhood was relieved. I ran into the Publix store manager at a local bar a few months after she moved away. I asked him how was business? He mentioned the woman by name and said patronage at the store was great since the EBT train was gone.

He Was a Strange One

I have worked with strange people throughout my career. We all have. There is one person that will remain in my memory that no purging could cleanse. His name was "Spot" and he was a strange one.

Spot was interviewed for a mechanical systems engineer position as a contract employee by the most senior Flight Test Engineer in the department. According to Karl, the interviewer, Spot said all the right things and it sounded as if he knew his stuff; but there was one thing that should have been a red flag: Spot had participated in the interview from a pay phone at a public library. Spot claimed there was construction occurring at his house and there would have been too much noise for the interview, that's why he was on a pay phone (This was when more people had landlines than mobile phones).

Spot seemed ok. He was five and half feet tall, in his early thirties and could have been considered a good-looking guy. Spot's first week on the job was to shadow his group leader, Seamus, so he would become familiar with his new responsibilities. Seamus wasn't impressed with Spot. Seamus told me that he didn't think Spot was capable of keeping up with the work and that Spot's attempts to use the data system were "pathetic." Coincidentally, I had just completed a series of fuselage pressure survey flight tests and I was going to need help plotting the data on time history graphs. I suggested giving Spot the assignment to plot the data. There was a huge amount of data. It would give Spot the practice he needed using the data system. Seamus liked the idea, so Spot was temporarily assigned to me.

I told Spot what I was expecting for the data formats and overall presentation. There were 50 pressure ports and twelve test conditions. A lot of data. He printed a sample sheet that was a very good initial attempt. I provided comments for improvements and requested he produce a second sample sheet. He went ahead and plotted all the data based on my first set of redlines. The final product was very good. I was impressed. He obviously mastered the data system, so I gave him back to Seamus to return to his original assignment.

The good times didn't last long. People started noticing that Spot was in the office when they arrived at the beginning of the day. The workday could start as early as an hour before sunrise for anyone supporting a flight test that needed the ideal weather conditions at the beginning of the day; otherwise, everyone started trickling in between 6:30 and 6:45AM. Spot would also disappear for a few hours at midday and always remained in the office past the usual office hours. He would log nine to ten hours a day. This attendance behavior drove Seamus crazy. Since Spot was a contract employee and Seamus was his supervisor, Seamus was responsible for approving his timecard, including overtime. Seamus stuck to a strict 6:30AM to 5:00PM work schedule and he did not want to deviate from his regimen to watch over Spot. Spot also started to log overtime on the weekends without getting prior approval. That also caused problems because there was not much testing for the Mechanical Systems team occurring at that time. The department was monitoring costs closely. A brake system test was scheduled a few months away that would eat a lot of funds. Being frugal now would allow greater than normal overtime later.

Other strange behaviors also emerged. Anyone chewing gum would set off Spot. He would hunch his shoulders and a look of intense pain would appear on his face anytime he heard someone chewing gum. He would brush his ears as if gnats were biting and say that he can't stand that noise. Then there was the musical chairs. Spot insisted there was something wrong with his chair. He would trade his desk chair for a conference room chair several times throughout the day. He would sit down, wiggle in his seat and mumbled something about the chair not feeling right. After he cycled through the conference room chairs, he would trade with someone that was away from their desk. Weeks later, he was placing a sheet of paper on his chair, insisting the chair was not clean. At first, he would take a clean sheet of paper from the copy machine tray to place over his seat. When a sheet outlived its usefulness, he moved it to the far corner of his desk. As the days wore on, Spot was increasing his paper seat cover use. It got to a point where he had a ream of copier paper on his desk and using one sheet at a time, cover the chair then discard the paper. Toward the end he was going through two reams of paper a day and the stack of used, crumpled paper surpassed ten inches in height.

Spot also surfed the internet too much. It was still the early days of the web and before the company had firewalls. Spot would complain that his computer would crash. Our local IT expert discovered Spot had chat rooms going on three or four different web browsers operating simultaneously causing the machine to run out of memory and lock up.

I had a strange conversation with Spot one Saturday, or more correctly, I listened to Spot talk about his life. On that Saturday morning, I stopped at the restaurant in the Days Inn Airport motel for breakfast. I was friends with the restaurant owner, so I ate there on occasion. His wife greeted me when I entered. I saw Spot sitting alone at a table near a window. I was curious why he was in this restaurant, and I wondered if he planned to go to the office that day. I knew he did not get approval for the weekend overtime. Spot noticed me when I hugged Michaela as

I entered. He perked up and motioned that I join him. He looked like he had been up all night. His eyes were bloodshot, and he was wearing the same clothes he had worn the previous day. He hadn't showered or shaved.

"Hi Spot, how are you doing?" I started the conversation.

He asked how I was and if I was heading into the office. He also asked why I was working on a Saturday. Then he asked why I was at that restaurant.

"The owner and his wife are friends of mine," I told him. He had nearly trembled when I said that and immediately had a look of someone caught doing something wrong. I mentioned his appearance. Spot said he had a rough night. He went to Uncle Harry's last night and stayed late. *Uncle Harry's was a topless bar near the river.* He said he was innocently caught in a commotion at the bar. The bouncers locked him in a storeroom for a few hours before tossing him out. He drove to the Days Inn but was too tired to check in to the motel, so he slept in his car. I asked about his apartment, but he said he moved out and had not found a suitable place yet. He had been staying at the Days Inn or the Quail Run Inn across the street.

While he was telling his story, Michaela brought my breakfast to the table. She was all smiles as she usually was. She turned to Spot with a serious expression and asked if he was ready for his ticket. Spot replied that he wasn't; he may order something additional. She said nothing and walked away.

I asked him why he was going to Uncle Harry's. He said he usually went there on the weekends, but after last night he was not welcome. He admitted there was a stripper that he was fond of. He then asked me about people at work. He wanted to know if I thought any of them would rent him a room. He wanted to know what coworkers thought of him. I lied telling him that no one had said anything to me about him. He also commented about his boss, Seamus. He liked him but he thought Seamus was being too terse with him. He then asked if any coworkers in the office had teenage daughters. That got my attention! I told him that he moved deep into the creepy realm with that question for which he apologized and blamed the comment on his lack of sleep. I was done with my breakfast and done with the conversation. I said I had to go to work and got up the leave. He said he would see me there in a few minutes. I told him he couldn't work today because I didn't see him on the approved overtime list. My final comment to Spot was that he should get some sleep.

Michaela waved me over when I left.

"You know that guy?" she asked.

I explained that he was a contract employee in my department and that he had only been with the company for a few weeks. She unloaded on me about Spot. He had been dining at the restaurant occasionally. Each time he would bypass the cashier on the way out; leaving money on the table without knowing what the correct amount was and always shortchanging the bill. There were two waitresses on her staff that were also dancers at Uncle Harry's (*they danced at night, then worked morning shift waitressing*). They told her that he stalked them at the club and followed them to the hotel restaurant weeks ago. She mentioned other weird behavior she heard about.

Two days later, Seamus called me over to his desk. "You've got to listen to this phone message," he chuckled.

Spot's voice played from the phone:

> Yeah Seamus. Hi. This is Spot. I was out last night. I got caught in the rain. I fell in a puddle. I took something and I woke up with my head like Mary Queen of Scots. Anyway, I won't been in. I'll call later. This is Spot.

"It didn't rain last night," I said.

123

"Mary, Queen of Scots," Seamus laughed, "What the fuck does that mean?"

Spot sealed his fate later that same week. Elsie, one of my young and hyper-talented engineers, approached me as soon as I arrived in the office. Elsie was very upset; she needed to tell me something immediately. She said she was in the office at 5:00AM to complete final preparations for a flight test she was to conduct at sunrise. She had been preparing flight cards for 20 minutes or so at her desk, then went into the library room for a handbook. She turned on the light for the room and saw a body on the floor covered in a blanket. It startled her. She screamed and ran to her desk. She was about to call security then realized it was Spot when he walked to the men's room with a moan. One of the aircraft mechanics entered the office and Elsie asked him to stay with her until more people arrived.

I looked over to Spot's desk. He was sitting there wearing the same clothes he had on when I saw him days ago at the restaurant. Elsie had calmed down a lot, but she said she didn't want to be alone in the office with him again. I asked if she was going to report it to the Employee Relations department. She replied that she was hoping that I would. Seamus arrived and we filled him in about Spot's sleeping in the library. Seamus and I told Elsie that we would support her discussion with Employee Relations, but Elsie backed down from reporting the incident claiming she didn't want anyone to get in trouble.

An idea came to me as how to solve the Spot problem. I had a dinner date with a friend that night. The friend lived near the office, so I would return to the office after the date to see if Spot was there.

After midnight, I returned to the office and saw lights on. I looked through a window to see Spot at his desk. He had a webpage open on his computer screen that showed a photo of a girl. I entered the building from a door that was diagonally opposite from where Spot's desk was located so he wouldn't immediately notice me entering. I walked around a corner appearing suddenly next to his desk. When Spot noticed me, he leapt from his chair and ran into the men's room. I looked at his computer screen, and sure enough, there was a chat page open along with several other webpages behind it.

Spot walked from the men's room attempting a casual stride as if he never saw me. "Oh, hey. What are you doing here?"

"What are you doing here?" I echoed back to him.

"Just trying to finish a project for Seamus. Don't worry, I'm not charging the company for any overtime," he said reaching to minimize the page on the screen.

"That didn't look like work, Spot," I said sternly. "It looked like you were surfing the web. What is it? A dating sight?"

"No man, I was doing real work. I just wanted to send a quick note to my girlfriend," he shot back, "What are you doing here so late?"

"I had a date. Forgot my meds in my desk. This was on my way home."

"Oh," he said with a dejected demeanor. He knew he was caught. He fidgeted in place wondering what to do next.

"Let's go. You look like you need sleep. Time to get out of here," I said gesturing toward the nearest exit. He collected a few personal items from his desk, then shuffled out the door. We walked together toward the parking lot.

Halfway to the guard gate, Spot said, "I forgot something. I've got to go back. Don't wait for me!" With that said, he ran back to the office.

I waited for a minute or two. I went back to look through the window again. Spot was there on his computer – the webpage with the girl was on the screen. I went to the guard gate and notified the security officer there was a contractor employee in my building misusing company assets. I also called the Director of Flight Test, waking him at 1AM, to inform him of Spot's behavior and needed his authority for Spot's immediate dismissal. The guard said he would escort Spot off the premises, but the termination would have to wait until the morning when the Human Resources and Security offices opened.

I got about four hours of sleep then I had to return to work to deal with the Spot mess. Back in the office, I told Seamus, Elsie and Karl about the previous night. Karl mentioned he saw Spot sleeping in his car in the parking lot when he arrived. A few minutes later, Spot entered the office escorted by a security guard. He was wearing the same clothes. He gathered a few things from his desk under the guard's watchful presence. Spot said goodbye to coworkers as he left.

"Sorry this didn't work out," I said to him and shook his hand.

"It's OK. These jobs usually last only three months anyway," he replied. He was escorted off the premises.

Ski Trip

In 1995, my family wanted to take a ski holiday between Christmas and the New Year. Sixteen months earlier, we lived in Southern California and my wife enjoyed skiing. She was not an avid skier, nor was she one to speed down the mountain. We had lived little more than an hour from Mountain High ski resort in Wrightwood. She talked a lot about taking the kids skiing, then when we moved to Georgia, that stopped the skiing discussions for a while.

It could have been through conversations with neighbors, or with soccer moms at a kid's match, or from adverts in local papers, my wife discovered there was skiing only six hours away in North Carolina. Skiing was back on the activities list. Once the kids heard about skiing, that's all I heard from the kids for weeks.

The day after Christmas Day, we packed up the truck, a 1991 GMC S-15 Jimmy, and drove to Boone, North Carolina. Ryan was ten years old, and Sarah was seven. We were barely out of Savannah, and they started with, "where's the snow?" and "are we there yet?" And the questioning continued for another five and a half hours.

We checked in to a Days Inn hotel within a few miles of the ski resort. My wife had reserved two days of skiing for her and the kids. *I didn't ski. Rheumatoid arthritis and sports injuries took their toll on my knees. For the previous eight years, my left knee had no cruciate ligaments, both completely torn/severed, and no meniscus tissue. I wouldn't have lasted five seconds on skis.* Both kids were enrolled in Ski Wee – a program to teach kids the basics of skiing. Ryan, always the daredevil, bragged about how he was going to graduate from Ski Wee on the first day. Sarah, super-competitive with her brother, boasted that she would too.

The next morning, we had breakfast at the hotel. The lady that operated the restaurant was cook, server, cashier and cleaning crew. Sarah and Ryan at that age could charm just about any adult out of candy, soda or ice cream, and they got this lady to give them free hot chocolate to go. The day got off to a good start for them. We arrived at the resort, and I dealt with the rental equipment: trousers, jackets, gloves, boots, skis, etc. I got the kids dressed while my wife dealt with her equipment. In earlier discussions, my wife had mentioned that it was a good idea to wear an article of clothing that was unique so it would be easier to spot her and the kids. She had chosen a long cone shaped hat with a white ball tip that went to her ankles (how it stayed on her head, I have no idea). Ryan had also selected a hat, but his was a red and blue chef style hat. Sarah was given a sky blue and pink stocking hat with a huge sky blue/pink puffball on top with matching scarf. After everyone was decked out, the kids went off to Ski Wee and my wife tried a few runs on the bunny slope for warm up prior to the intermediate level run. I looked around the resort. There was an ice rink for skating – good family event for the night. The resort building was called the Swiss Chalet for some reason that was not obvious to me. I found a few places where I could sit and read and watch the skiers. I had an 8mm video camera so I could record everyone in action -- finding the right place was important.

Every now and then, I would be in the base area between the Swiss Chalet and the ski lift for the diamond run to video record Ryan and Sarah in Ski Wee. I was surprised that Ski Wee taught kids skiing fundamentals without poles. Within two hours, the senior Ski Wee instructor approached me and told me that Ryan didn't need Ski Wee. He was a natural, probably as good as any of the instructors; so, Ryan was dismissed from Ski Wee and joined his mom on the intermediate slopes.

Sarah complained that she wanted to ski with her brother. I told her that she had to finish Ski Wee and if the instructor told me at the end of the day that she graduated, then she could ski with her brother tomorrow. Sarah made graduating from Ski Wee her only goal. Meanwhile, Ryan was mastering the intermediate slopes. He was speed skiing back and forth without poles, trying to do tricks each time he got air under his skis. His mother leisurely skied from side to side as she made her way down the slope. On a few occasions, Ryan would speed by her and do a loop around her.

After the lunch break, Ski Wee moved to the bunny slope. The "lift" for the bunny slope was a looped rope driven by a flywheel. It was entertaining watching the small six and seven year old kids attempting to grab the rope. Most only made it five or ten feet up the slope before being thrown off the rope, ending in a face plant into the snow or flipping on their back. By the third attempt, they were able to hang on to the top of the hill. Sarah's natural ability began to show. She would fly down the bunny slope without zigging or zagging down the hill. She was as much a speed demon as her brother. She liked to extend her arms straight out as if they were wings as she skied. The Ski Wee instructor was on her to avoid going straight down and turn more often to avoid other skiers, but she didn't care. When she saw her mom or her brother finishing a run, she would ski off the bunny slope to meet them at the line for the lift, attempting to join them on their next run.

Ryan had moved to the diamond slope. He was flying down the slopes, trying to outski everyone. He also terrorized the snowboarders. When he saw a snowboarder cut off his mom or another skier, he would tuck to gain speed then cut in front of the boarder.

When Ski Wee was over for the day, the instructor told me that Sarah was ready to ski on her own. I had Sarah show me everything she learned in Ski Wee along with two or three runs down the bunny slope to show me that she could do it. She didn't know I was watching and recording her all day.

"Ok," I said, "Next time Mommy appears we will see if she will take you on the intermediate slope."

Ryan came flying around a corner, face flush from cold wind and panting heavily.

"Ryan!" Sarah cried, "Daddy said I can ski diamond!" as she waddled toward her brother. Their mom drifted over, and Sarah waddled in her direction. Sarah begged to ski on a slope with her.

"Ok, we'll try the blue circle run. Ryan will ski with us," she said. "We'll ski two or three more runs then we will be done for today," she said to me.

I went to the upper deck of the Swiss Chalet to video record them during their runs. Each run became a race between Ryan and Sarah as to who would finish first. When they were done, Ryan wanted to have one final go at the diamond slope. Sarah wanted to accompany her brother, but her mom said they would wait at the bottom to watch Ryan. He flew down the slope without poles in his speediest run of the day. Ryan felt like Superman and wanted to show off.

That night we walked to a barbecue restaurant just down the road from the hotel. Although I didn't ski, I was tired from carrying equipment and walking all over the resort recording video. The restaurant had an open sports bar layout. There was a guitar duo on a dais singing a mixture of rock and country songs. To me, they sounded like an old country-rock band from Chicago known as Mason Proffitt. At one time in the evening, I asked if they knew of the band and the older guitarist replied, "Hell yeah. Jerry Talbot. I know 'Two Hangmen'." The other guitarist didn't know the song. I told them I did, and they let me sit in playing the bass part on a guitar. My family gave a loud applause. My three skiers were tired but famished. It was one of those rare times when I didn't have to push either kid to finish what was on their plate.

It started snowing while we were in the restaurant. When we returned to the hotel, there was at least two inches of snow in the parking lot. I couldn't help beaning my wife in the back of the head with a soft snowball. That prompted a snowball fight among the four of us that lasted about an hour. After everyone was tucked in for the night, I sat in a lounge chair sipping blackberry brandy for 30 minutes before retiring.

It continued snowing throughout the night. When I awoke the next morning there was nearly two feet of new snow. The kids were all excited. Sarah was already talking about skiing the diamond slope. The family got dressed quickly. I tried to slow them down because I knew the roads were not plowed yet. I was concerned about road conditions. It had been a while since I had to do any real winter driving and my Jimmy was only a rear wheel drive SUV, but I didn't want to dampen their mood about skiing. The restaurant in the hotel opened about an hour late because the manager couldn't make it in due to the road conditions. She had a full house of customers that were antsy to get to the mountain and it fouled her mood.

The main road was plowed as I started the drive to the ski resort. The road trail to the resort was not. I was doing ok in the deep snow until I came to the last steep hill before the resort. Traction was a challenge as I started up the slope. I had to hush the kids from their loud stories, telling them I needed to concentrate on driving. About halfway up, the back end of the truck began to skid toward the edge of the road.

The day before I noticed there was no guardrail on this part of the road and only a few inches of shoulder followed by a long drop down the mountain. My wife and the kids noticed my difficulty keeping the vehicle in control. They started to panic as the Jimmy slid down the slope backwards. I told my wife to climb over the seats into the bed of the SUV and sit over the rear axle and to take the kids with her. I downshifted to first gear. With the added weight over the rear axle, I regained control and slowly inched up the mountain.

At the Swiss Chalet, the family donned their rented ski equipment. Sarah pestered her mom the whole time "I want to go on the diamond!" The chalet common room was filled to capacity with skiers preparing for the day on the slopes. A voice over the PA said, "Good morning, everyone. As you know, we received several inches of snow last night. We need to check the slopes before we open them for skiing."

Three snowmobiles with skiers riding along passed by the glass doors of the chalet. "The ski patrol just went out to check the slopes. When they radio back with favorable news, we will start the lifts. They will need to run for ten minutes before we will allow passengers onto the lifts. Please stand by for another 30 minutes."

A groan of anticipation was released by everyone in the common room. Ryan was dancing in place with anticipation. Sarah kept tugging on her mom's coat.

"Can I go on the diamond with you and Ryan?" she asked for the hundredth time.

"Yes, fine!" Mom exclaimed. "Leave me alone!"

A pair of skiers in day-glow yellow vests with PATROL across the chest appeared from the snowy slopes. The ski lifts came on. The crowd gave a roar of approval knowing they would be allowed to ski in a few minutes. I was about to tell Ryan to keep an eye on his sister throughout the day when I noticed Sarah was gone.

"Where's Sarah?" I asked.

"I don't know. Where is she?" my wife replied. She called for Sarah in the common room. She was nowhere to be found. We asked the others waiting to ski if they saw a little girl with a pink and sky blue hat with matching scarf. Others started looking with us. Then we heard a woman say, "Look, there is a kid on the ski lift!"

I looked toward the lift and saw two little skis dangling below a bench on the lift chair rising toward the top of the hill. Oh shit.

"She's on the ski lift for the diamond slope," I told my wife. "Go tell the management."

I told Ryan to go to the lift operator's station to tell them Sarah was on the lift.

I pulled the camera out of its pack as I ran up to the top deck of the chalet. I heard my wife scream at the Ski Patrol that her daughter was on the lift to the diamond run. I positioned myself on the deck to have the clearest view to the top of the slope. Sarah was two-thirds of the way to the top of the slope, her feet kicking in excitement and the pink/sky blue puffball on her hat bobbing above the back of the bench. The three snowmobiles that had returned a few minutes earlier to the chalet zoomed by heading up the slope. They weren't going to make it in time to intercept her. I used the camera zoom to its max setting as if it was a telescope to follow Sarah's progress in the lift. The bench she was riding disappeared over the top of the hill. The ski patrol was still struggling up the slope on the deep snow. A tiny figure glided into view at the top of the run. With max zoom, she was no bigger than a match head held at arm's length, but I could barely make out the pink and sky blue hat and a smile on her face. She thrust her arms straight out like airplane wings and began her descent down the hill…

Sarah was coming straight down the hill. She didn't turn, zig or zag. Straight down with arms out, ankles together, knees locked, gaining speed. I followed her as she sped on her downward trajectory with the camera, now zooming out. My heart skipped a beat when her legs spread apart on two occasions, but she stayed up. Halfway down, she hit a hidden mogul. I thought she was a goner. I pictured in my mind of her landing face first into the snow breaking her neck, but she landed with her knees locked as if she was landing on cotton. Sarah picked up more speed as she headed straight for the chalet. She was going so fast, I thought she was going to crash into the side of the building, and I heard her mother gasp as if she predicted the same thing. Sarah entered the base area faster than any skier I saw the previous day. When she was only a few feet away from the gathered crowd, she torqued herself 90 degrees to stop, showering her mom, brother and the ski patrol in snow.

"That was fun, Mommy! I want to do it again,' Sarah exclaimed, then waved up to me as she waddled toward the ski lift.

Epilogue: We received a lecture from the resort management. They asked us to leave, but after I explained about this being the kids first time, etc. and their Ski Wee instructor saying that both Ryan and Sarah were excellent skiers, the management let us stay for the remainder of the day. Only after all three repeated the ski rules. I also dropped a 'Grant' on his desk during the explanation. Maybe it helped.

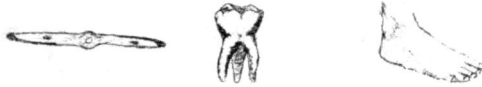

College Pranks

I attended college at Parks College of St. Louis University or simply known as "Parks." Parks was located in Cahokia, Illinois at a former US Army Air Corps training camp since the college's inception through to the year 2000. Cahokia wasn't one of the most metropolitan places in Illinois. It was in the St. Louis metro area with East St. Louis and Sauget to the north and Belleville eight miles to the east. Unless you could drive across the river to St. Louis, there wasn't much locally to keep several hundred aviation students entertained.

Student pranks occurred often at Parks, as they did at other college campuses, but I believe the pranks at Parks were some of the greatest in college history. The pranks could be divided into two categories: graduation pranks and rivalry pranks. Graduation pranks occurred at the end of each semester. The graduating class, sometimes with help from non-graduating senior students, would perform their prank the night before the graduation ceremony. Each graduating class would try to outperform the previous class.

Some memorable graduation pranks that occurred during my senior year included seeing Dr. Manor's desk on top of the Holloran Hall dormitory. Dr. Manor was an Aerodynamics professor from Israel. He was accustomed to the traditional old world style university dynamics where professors rarely interacted with students, whereas the Parks student-professor dynamic was similar to the American student-teacher high school experience. His most overused expression was "I will not spoon feed you" when students asked too many questions. I remember his desk on the roof with a sheet tied to the side facing the quad with **I WILL NOT SPOON FEED YOU** spray-painted on the sheet. What was funnier was how the desk kidnappers entered the professor's office through the ceiling ventilation ducting in the middle of the night so as not to commit forcible entry through the office door.

The next class pranked the Wind Tunnel laboratory. The wind tunnel lab had a supersonic tunnel that used a huge air tank mounted outside the lab for the compressed air required to generate supersonic airflow in the test section of the tunnel. The air tank was over 10 feet long and at least six feet in diameter. The night before the graduation ceremony several students painted the air tank into the semblance of a giant Busch beer can laying on its side. I contributed (although I was not in the graduating class that semester) by calculating the volume of the tank and painting 2.7×10^5 FLUID OUNCES on the tank.

My graduating class pulled a prank that required a crane to reverse it. The night before graduation, I ran into Dave, a fellow graduating senior, as I walked to STOOGES, the bar next to campus. I offered to buy the first round of beer, but he said not until we pulled off senior prank. I asked him what he had in mind. His plan was to relocate all the aircraft fuselage sections in the structures lab onto the roof of McDonnell Douglas Hall. That would be one hell of a prank because there were four fuselage sections in the lab, but there was no way only he and I could do it. We recruited eight students drinking at STOOGES for assistance. It took about 20 minutes to move a Cessna 402 fuselage section out of the lab and onto the roof of the lab building; all the while avoiding security guards and two professors that were still in the building. The Cessna section was the wing-body piece that included the wing spars and engine mounts. We positioned the section nose down on the roof of McDonnell Douglas Hall. Dave spray-painted a pair of eyes and a smile on the top of the fuselage. The next morning the campus was covered in dense fog. As the fog slowly dispersed, the prank looked like a huge silver spider on top of the building.

Graduation pranks were fun; the rivalry pranks were better.

One day there were flyers scattered throughout the campus stating **BE ON THE LOOKOUT FOR CAPTAIN COMMIE!** A visit from Captain Commie was similar to a streaker, but without the nudity. Two students came up with the idea. They took turns dressing in a red body suit, red cape and a red eye cover mask. When dressed as the Captain, the student would run across the quad, through the cafeteria and through one or two classroom buildings before disappearing into the bean field next to campus. Harmless. Stupid. Funny (sort of).

A more daring prank was to steal the license plate off an Illinois State patrol car parked in the apartment complex next to the campus where many students lived. After eight plates were creatively appropriated, the prank was declared too easy.

One day, the AHP propeller disappeared. Alpha Eta Rho (AHP) was a professional fraternity with a chapter at Parks College. Back in the 1930's, the charter members of the Parks chapter removed a wooden Hartzell propeller from a biplane at the nearby Bi-State Parks airport, but they left a lot of cash in the cockpit to compensate the owner. The propeller remained in the fraternity ever since. The prop was usually displayed in the chapter president's dorm room during his term. It was an annual prank for the AHP pledge class to "steal" the prop and return it with a new layer of wax. But on this occasion, it was not the AHP pledge class that took the prop. It was removed from the dorm room by a rival fraternity and hidden in the backseat of a car. The unsuspecting car owner drove to St. Louis to hang out with friends. He noticed the prop in the backseat and asked his friend to keep it at his house for a while. After a week, the AHP president declared at a meeting of the Greek Council that the police would be notified if the prop was not returned within 24 hours. The 60 year old propeller was worth thousands of dollars and it had been moved across the Illinois-Missouri state line, making the appropriation a felony if it was declared a theft. The next day, the propeller appeared in an oak tree on the campus quad.

A podiatrist opened an office down the road from the campus with a sculpture of a large foot mounted by the entrance. If that wasn't an open invitation for trouble, then nothing was. Very soon the toenails were covered with purple paint. Then the foot had bunions and corns. Then it was wrapped in toilet paper like an ace bandage.

A few months after the podiatrist opened his office, a dentist opened an office next door. The dentist hadn't paid attention to what happened to his neighbor and mounted a large tooth sculpture in front of his office. And sure enough within a few days, the large molar had a cavity. A few days later, the cavity received a filling. Then the tooth developed tartar.

The best prank involved a Taco Bell restaurant. Back in the 1980's, Taco Bell restaurants had a real bell in the belfry above the entrance. The Taco Bell in Cahokia was about a mile from campus. Back then, the Taco Bell didn't have a drive through. It was purely an indoor dining establishment that closed by 10PM each day. In my second to last semester at Parks, I decided to pull the ultimate prank: get the bell from Taco Bell.

One of my friends was a student named Roy who worked with his father restoring cars. Roy had a 1967 Camaro that was restored beautifully. He also had a 1970 Ford E350 utility truck with an amber paint job and an old amber rotating light on the roof. Roy and I drove his truck to Taco Bell, set up orange cones around the truck and propped a ladder against the building. I climbed to the belfry and proceeded to remove the bell. Roy stayed on the ground, wearing a hard hat, keeping cars and people away while I worked. I was about halfway done when the restaurant manager came outside demanding to know what we were doing. I told him we were sent from the regional office to replace the store's bell. The manager claimed he knew nothing about the bell replacement. I told him that I couldn't stop to argue with him; we had three more stores to visit that day. I also told him to get the paperwork from the regional office because I would need it when I brought the replacement bell. The manager told us he would make some calls and that we shouldn't leave. He went back into the restaurant in a huff. Roy scrambled up the ladder with ropes to help me finish the removal. We lowered the bell onto the truck and hauled ass out of there.

That night, Roy and I were watching the news while admiring our new trophy. The local news segment usually contained items about downtown St. Louis, but this night they featured the Taco Bell in Cahokia. A reporter interviewed the restaurant manager we encountered, who proceeded to tell the story about how the bell was taken from his store. The segment finished with a "if you have any details about the theft, please call..." Damn! There goes our trophy.

Roy and I talked about disposing the bell. Dump it in the river or abandon it in the bean field or leave it at the airport were options. All scenarios were unappealing to me. We pulled off the best prank ever. I didn't want to give it up so quickly.

The next night, members of the Alpha Beta Gamma (ABΓ) fraternity were having a party at a house they rented on the other side of town. I formulated a plan for what to do with the bell that depended on the predictability of the Gamma guys and the Cahokia police force.

Back in 1986, Cahokia had a population of around 15,000 people, not including the Parks students living on campus. The police department had maybe 12 officers with usually no more than three officers on duty during late night.

On party night, Roy and I loaded the bell into his utility truck along with all the ropes, tools and ladders. We parked the truck on campus in the loading area of the maintenance shop. We took his Camaro to the Gamma party and hung out until 10PM. I remember holding the same cup full of beer that was handed to me when we arrived without taking a sip. If my plan worked, we would drink later. Since this Taco Bell

139

didn't have a drive through, it closed by 10PM on Fridays and weekends. We left the Gamma party shortly after 10PM. We got the truck and drove to a pay phone near the Taco Bell and waited for another hour. Around 11:30PM, I called the police department pretending to be a neighbor complaining about the noise coming from a party full of college students. As I hoped, within a few minutes all three police cruisers were heading to the other side of town with their light bars sending blue strobes into the street.

The Taco Bell was empty and dark when we arrived. As a bonus for us, the parking lot was unlit. It took us about 20 minutes to re-install the bell in its belfry. We drove back to campus, swapped vehicles, then drove back to the Gamma party. By the time we got there, the party had been dispersed by the police. Roy and I walked up to the house asking Pablo, the Gamma chapter president and renter of the house, what happened?

"Some neighbor called the cops on us. We weren't that loud. Just a load of B.S.," Pablo said. "Where have you been?"

We told him of the Taco Bell caper but left out the part of calling the police.

Within ten years of the great Taco Bell caper, all the Taco Bell restaurants had plastic bell facades mounted above their buildings. The original metal bells and brick belfries had gone. Sometimes I wonder if it is because of a pair of bored college students in Cahokia, Illinois…

Kathy & the Secret Agent

There was a lounge near the Savannah International Airport called "Bailey's Cockpit" located at the Days Inn Airport motel. The "Cockpit" was a round building on top of pilings in the retention pond in front of the motel. A wooden walkway spanned 30 feet of water from the parking lot to the deck that wound around the circumference of the building. Inside, three-quarters of the building was the lounge with a square bar in the center. Polarized glass from floor to ceiling provided a panoramic view of the pond and the airport. A jukebox was near the entrance, and a Cruzin' USA arcade booth was next to the emergency exit directly opposite of the entrance. The remaining one-quarter of the building was the kitchen and restrooms.

The Cockpit was my regular place for lunch during the mid to late 1990's. Many longtime patrons sat at the same table or same spot at the bar – I was no exception. I always sat on the side of the bar between the cash register and the flip-up door, facing the entrance. I'd spend about 45 minutes having my lunch while talking to the owner, Robyn, or one of the staff. All the bartenders and waitresses were female, as was one of the cooks. The only male on staff was another cook named Tommy. He was a young black man, tall and thin, already losing his hair that he kept under a red baseball cap with the bill flipped upward. Tommy had a large gap between his front teeth with a neutral facial expression similar to the character "Bubba" from the movie *Forrest Gump*.

Two interesting staff members were Kathy and Kim. Both were very beautiful ladies. Kathy was tall and busty with an athletic build, topped with long auburn hair. Kim was blonde and busty, shorter than Kathy, and also athletic. Neither had a filter when they spoke, so they provided a lot of entertainment when they worked. Both were featured in the Cockpit's bikini calendar for three consecutive years. Kathy was always struggling with financial problems. Kim was married and spent more time terrorizing the streets of Savannah in her collection of Nissan Z-model cars than with her husband.

During one lunch break at the Cockpit, a man walked in wearing a silver Armani double breasted suit, an expensive pair of brown leather shoes and a pork pie hat. This was an unusual sight to see on a hot and humid summer day. The man selected a stool at the bar. Kathy was bartending that day. When she turned toward him to take his order, he did a small double take motion with his head. He fished a pack of cigarettes out of his jacket pocket as he ordered a club soda. He smoked his cigarette, sipping his club soda while scanning the lounge. When he finished his cigarette, he offered to pay his tab with a $100 bill. Kathy decided not to charge him for the soft drink because of the large bill. He pocketed his money and cigarettes and left.

Two days later, he showed up at the Cockpit during lunch time again wearing the same outfit. He went to the same stool as before. Kim was tending bar, but he noticed Kathy bussing a recently vacated table, to where he promptly relocated. He sipped a club soda while smoking a cigarette and made small talk with Kathy. When he finished his cigarette, he again tried to close his tab with a $100 bill, but Kathy negated the tab and he left.

Kim mentioned that she thought he was a strange fellow and asked Kathy what he talked about. Kathy said that he said he was some kind of agent working with a government task force. He said a few other things that she didn't understand. Kathy thought it was no big deal –

guys were bullshitting her all the time, why would this guy be any different?

A few days later, I was in the Cockpit for lunch. A red and silver Dodge Colt pulled into the parking lot. Robyn and Kim giggled; Kathy let out a groan.

"Hey Dennis, did you see what Kathy's new secret agent boyfriend is driving?" Robyn asked jokingly as he walked by my seat. The man in the silver Armani suit got out the car.

"He's been coming in on the days that Kathy is scheduled to work," Robyn said, "I tell her she has a stalker."

"I'm starting to believe you," Kathy added. "I shouldn't have taken the $100 from him."

"That's new info. Why did you take money from him?" asked Robyn.

"He only orders club soda, then tries to pay with a $100 bill. I tell him to keep his money, but one time he told me to keep the $100 and I really needed the money."

"Way to go Kathy," I said, "you fed a stray cat. You won't be able to get rid of him."

"He talks about how he's scouting the area along with the CIA. He says the Pope is going to visit the area and terrorists are going to try to kill him."

"Why does he come here? Does he think the Pope is going come in for a beer and buy a calendar? Or ask you and Kim to autograph your pictures?"

Kathy snickered with that comment, then turned to hand the secret agent a menu. He went through his routine with the club soda and smoking a cigarette, engaged in small talk with Kathy, then left. She said he talked about the plot against the Pope again but no new details. I suggested to Robyn that she should make sure one or two trusted patrons escort her to her car on the nights she closes while this "secret agent" is around. He agreed.

The following Saturday, I was working and stopped at the Cockpit for lunch before I headed home. It was near midafternoon with overcast skies. What started as a slight drizzle turned into a typical coastal Georgia summer thunderstorm. I was the only customer in the Cockpit. Kathy was the sole person working the lounge and Tommy was in the kitchen. After she took my order, Kathy jumped into the Cruzin' USA arcade machine. Robyn, Tommy, Kim and Kathy were addicted to the game since the machine arrived. It was entertaining watching them play as they would lean to the right or left from the visual cues on the screen. Kathy let out a few F-bombs and S-bombs as she drove her virtual Lamborghini through the streets of Los Angeles. She finished her round as Tommy brought my food from the kitchen. Then it was his turn at the game. Tommy chose a school bus as his racing vehicle. It was suitable for him as I could easily picture Tommy driving 80 miles per hour through Compton in a fish-tailing school bus.

The rain poured heavily for a while. When it let up, I decided to leave before another downpour occurred. I was pocketing my change when Kathy pointed toward the parking lot and asked me not to leave. The red and silver Dodge Colt pulled into the lot. The secret agent had arrived. I told Kathy that I would stay, and she calmed down a bit. The secret agent, wearing the same Armani suit, shoes, and pork pie hat as before, entered the bar. He scanned the lounge looking as if he was counting how many people were there. He sat at his usual stool. Kathy presented a menu. He ordered his usual club soda and fished for a pack of cigarettes. He leaned forward to engage in small talk with Kathy, but she stepped away. Kathy strode through the flip up door on the bar to stand beside me as I sat in my usual place. She leaned against me placing her arm across my shoulders. I wasn't expecting that, and neither was Tommy with a quizzical look on his face as he walked past us out the emergency exit for some fresh air.

"Come talk to us," Kathy said to the secret agent. She then looked at me, "he says he needs my help."

I immediately understood what Kathy was doing. She was trying to get the secret agent to believe that we were a couple, so I placed my arm around her waist.

"What's your story?" I asked.

"I was telling Kathy that I need her help," he said in a fake Italian tough-boy voice. He was agitated that I was now involved in the discussion. He got off his stool, taking a few steps in our direction. He was about five feet, eight inches tall. He held his club soda in his right hand and his cigarette between the index and middle fingers of his left hand. My martial arts training kicked in as I was assessing his stance and concluding that he was left-handed. His double-breasted suit was tight under his right armpit, suggesting to me there was something in an inside pocket or maybe something strapped to his side.

"I'm working with the CIA and Interpol," he explained, "The Pope will be in the area in a few days. Iranian terrorists are going to assassinate him."

"Why do you need her help?" I asked.

"Well, let me tell you." He paused and began checking his pockets. He unbuttoned the top two buttons of his jacket, reached inside with his left hand and pulled out a pack of cigarettes. With his jacket partially unbuttoned, I could see the butt of a handgun under his right arm. He opened the pack and proceeded to light a cigarette.

"May I have one?" I asked, getting up from my stool.

"Sure." He extended his right arm toward me. I stepped forward, grabbing the lapel of his suit with my left hand, reached into his suit and removed the gun with my right hand. In a continuous motion, I swung my right arm around to toss the gun through the open emergency exit door into the pond, narrowly missing Tommy as he was walking back in.

The secret agent was completely surprised. I pushed him backward against a table. I placed my forearm across his neck, leaning my weight onto his throat.

"You get out of here or I'll have Tommy pack you in the freezer."

He tried to lift my forearm off his throat, but I began to push more of my weight on him. He flailed his arms clearly giving up. I dragged him by his suit to the front entrance and threw him out onto the wet walkway. He landed face first, sliding several feet on the wet wood. He leapt to his feet then ran to his car. He tore out of the parking lot, running through a red light making a left turn onto the main road. Within seconds, a police car was in pursuit.

"Oh my God, he had a gun," Kathy sighed.

"I think it may have been a pellet gun," I replied. "It didn't seem heavy enough to be a handgun. And I'm not going to fish it out of the pond to find out."

"Damn Dennis, I guess you put the Pope outta danger," Tommy concluded.

We never saw the secret agent man again.

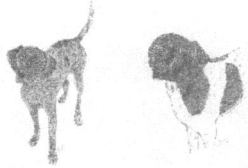

Dog Adoption II

As previously mentioned, I love dogs. I am partial to sporting and working breeds. I like herding dogs and I tolerate hounds. Terriers and toys provide no appeal to me. Years ago, I had a pair of Rottweilers – Artos and Morgan. They were incredible canine companions.

Morgan had an "American" Rottweiler appearance. Her head was slim with a long nose. She was light on her feet for a 90 pound Rottweiler. At bedtime, both dogs would curl up on their pillows, but once she sensed I was asleep, she would jump on the bed without shaking the bed or waking me. Although, she would wake me in the middle of the night by stretching or twitching in her sleep – paws scraping on my leg or back. She was the boss of Artos. She would mount him, trapping him against the edge of the pool or in the corner of the fence, taking away his dignity. She was very matronly too. Morgan cleaned Artos' ears several times a day. He would complain by crying and squirming, but Morgan would lay on him, flip open an ear with her nose and insert inches of tongue into his ear canal. You could almost feel the pain of the tongue going in your own ear as you were watching Artos deal with the cleaning. Licking was Morgan's way to express her love. I received minutes of her licks when she sensed I was stressed or injured.

Artos was a classic "German" Rottweiler with a wide head. At his heaviest he was 140 pounds. He had a very majestic appearance. His muscles rippled when he walked. Both dogs loved to stalk and chase squirrels when they were adolescents. When a squirrel scrambled up a tree, Artos would leap up in the air looking like a black school bus popping a wheelie. One leap resulted in torn knee ligaments and a fracture. Artos had canine knee replacement surgery along with follow-on swimming therapy. Thankfully, both lost interest in squirrels after that incident. Artos loved kids. Rottweilers usually do not tolerate their paws being touched or their docked tail messed with (their 'nubby' as the kids used to call it). Kids would lay on top of Artos, pull on his paws or his nubby but he seemed to enjoy it. He was hyper-protective of his family. I had to put him in the house whenever the pool was being used, otherwise he would grab your hand in his mouth and pull you out of the pool. I tested him to see how far he would go. I was in the deep end of the pool, splashing around calling for help. Artos pulled my seven foot, 260 pound frame out of the pool in two seconds. When guests stayed the night, he would lay in the doorway of the guest room, facing the hallway. He was going to guard his guest all night long.

Sadly, both passed away within 5 months of each other. Morgan went first. She lost her appetite and became lethargic. The vet x-rayed Morgan and performed urine and blood tests. X-rays did not show anything out of the ordinary. The other tests showed that her liver functions were failing. The vet suggested that she perform exploratory surgery; if she saw something out of the ordinary, she would remove it. Normally, both dogs went everywhere together, but I left Artos at home the day of the procedure. I handed Morgan over to the clinic technicians, loving on her as she looked at me with sad, tired eyes. About 45 minutes after I left Morgan, I received a call from the vet requesting I return to the clinic. Morgan was on the operating table laying on her back with her belly open, organs exposed. The vet showed me Morgan's spleen. It was covered with cancer. Her liver also had the gray cancer covering half the organ. The vet said Morgan was within a day or two of dying. I hugged Morgan and kissed her ears. I injected the sodium pentothal given to me by the vet into the IV. I said goodbye.

It was a sad drive home. The day became melancholier as I packed Morgan's collar away. Saddest of all was watching Artos realize Morgan was not coming home. He searched every room looking for her. He smelled my shirt longingly; it had her scent from when I hugged her. That night, he pulled the shirt out of the clothes hamper and slept with it for days.

Artos was in a funk for three weeks. He was clearly depressed. I took him everywhere with me as often as I could. He eventually accepted Morgan's departure, but he never returned to the happy, joyful Artos from before. Four months later, his health began a slow descent. He became easily fatigued. After getting up, he would cough and breathe heavily for a few seconds before he would walk. He needed to rest after climbing the three stairs from the yard to the back porch. When he was healthy, he had a funny way of laying down: planting his butt, then sliding his front legs forward. Now he simply collapsed. The vet performed x-rays and blood tests. The blood tests were normal. The x-rays suggested his heart was enlarged. The vet suggested smaller portions at feeding time along with adding fish oil to his diet and return in three weeks. Artos continued his decline. The day before his next vet visit, I had to carry him up the back porch stairs to get in the house. He couldn't cope with strain to his system. Another set of x-rays showed he had tumors on his heart. The vet did a needle probe into a tumor. The tumors were benign, but the damage was done. It was unlikely Artos would have survived a surgery to remove the tumors. He was struggling too hard to exist. I had to let him go. I sat on the floor of the examination room with Artos' head on my lap as the vet injected the sodium pentothal. He looked up at me as his breathing slowed. He let out a final gasp. I sat with him for a long time. I picked him up and carried him to another room for the technicians to prepare him for cremation. I took off his collar and left.

I had not felt such deep sadness as I did with his loss. I swore that I would never have another dog again. I didn't want to go through that pain again.

Five months later, my neighbors Alex and Fielding approached me with an awkward request. A member of their church had a litter of pointer puppies. There was a problem with the litter, some pups died. Since I raised bird dogs in the past, would I be willing to help this person? I said I would help if I could, so they put me in contact with a gentleman named Geert. I phoned Geert, telling him of my experience raising English Pointers and English Setters; and of the time I participated in Field Trialing with my uncle and cousin. Geert invited me to his home to view the puppies and make a judgement about their health. His dog, the mother, had a bad gastrointestinal infection during the latter half of the pregnancy. Birthing the litter was a struggle. Two pups were stillborn. Another survived for about a week before dying. Only two remained and he was uncertain if they would make it.

I went to his home. He let the mother and two surviving puppies into his yard. I examined the mother first. She was a small German Shorthair Pointer with a heavily ticked liver colored coat named Greta. She looked fine but her teats looked like she stopped nursing for nearly a week. That wasn't good because the puppies were only four to five weeks old.

Pointers are one of the most robust and hardy dog breeds in existence. They can handle heat, cold, or pain with incredible resilience. A pointer can be ill and the owner be unaware until it's too late. The German Shorthair Pointer is probably the most extreme of all the Pointer breeds.

The larger puppy was mainly white with big liver colored spots and a liver head. She was the more dominant of the two. Geert's granddaughter called her Trouble. I felt around her belly and ribs. Her puppy teeth were coming in ok. Her legs were wet. Geert said Trouble was incontinent. Trouble was constantly drinking water and urinating.

The smaller puppy looked identical to the mother and was called Mischief. She had vomited twice while playing. Geert said he had to begin transferring the puppies' nutrition to semi-solid food because Greta was reducing her nursing and Mischief was vomiting shortly after consuming food. Despite the digestion issues, Mischief appeared to have normal puppy energy, but Geert said Mischief would collapse from exhaustion soon.

I asked if their pointing instinct began. Geert produced a pole with a fishing line attached to one end. The opposite end of the string had a quail wing tied to it. He dangled the wing in the air, catching the puppies' attention. He placed the wing on the ground about ten feet away from the dogs. Both puppies froze in place looking directly at the wing. Mischief was crouched with her head down and one paw up and tucked back with her tail high in a classic pointer pose. Trouble stood tall with her tail up and ears at full attention. Greta was also pointing from across the yard. The puppies had a strong instinct, and their illness was not having a deterring effect on it. That was a good sign.

I asked Geert what a veterinarian had said about the puppies' health. Geert replied that he had not taken the puppies to a vet. He wanted to get their tails docked within a week of their birth, but he decided to wait to see if they would survive. He suspected Greta somehow passed her infection to the puppies in utero. I agreed. Geert then asked if I would take the puppies for a week to nurse them back to health. He didn't want his granddaughter to watch another puppy die and he already put a lot of money into the litter with sire fees and didn't want any more financial losses.

I thought about it for a while as we watched the puppies play. I wasn't ready to have dogs again. This was a request to foster the dogs for what could be their last days of life if any treatment I could devise did not work. I concluded that if these dogs were as sick as Geert believed, they'd die within a week; or if I could get them to hold down food, they should be recovered in a week. We agreed that I would take the puppies for a week and either return two healthy puppies or dispose of the dead animals for him.

When I got home, I turned the puppies loose in my yard which was over four times larger than their previous play area. They explored everywhere while I told my wife about the agreement I made with Geert. She had been nagging me since the day Artos died that she wanted another dog, specifically a miniature dachshund. I love dogs, but I'm not fond of ankle biting breeds. She thought these two were beautiful, adorable pups; but she didn't like 'Trouble' or 'Mischief' as names. She wanted to rename them. I reminded her that they were being fostered for a week and that neither of us should develop a bond with the puppies. I knew that giving them new names was the first step toward a greater commitment, but that wife rarely valued my input anyway. Trouble became Zoë. Mischief became Chloë.

Zoë's and Chloë's cuteness was a key factor in my wife's willingness to aide them. I told her a true story from my childhood about a family friend whose female pointer died birthing 16 pups. My mother and we kids helped with the feeding and cleanup of the litter. I couldn't remember what the milk mixture was that we fed the puppies for their first four weeks of life, but I did remember that when their baby teeth were emerging at around four weeks of age, they were fed a semi-solid food concoction called "Baby Birddog Food." The ingredients for Baby Birddog Food were cottage cheese, hard boiled eggs, white rice and cod liver oil. It had a rank odor when it was all blended together, but the puppies devoured it.

I thought one tablespoon of Baby Birddog Food every three hours for Zoë and Chloë would be a good start for a day or two. Just like the litter from over 35 years ago, these two devoured the Baby Birddog Food. Within minutes, Chloë regurgitated half of what she ate. Zoë handled the food better but drank a lot of water. She went running through the yard with a steady stream of urine coming out of her. Zoë's bladder was probably undersized or incompletely developed because of the infection passed on from her mother. After the third feeding of the day, Chloë held down her food! Big wins start with small victories…

The day ended with both puppies on my lap, curled up within themselves. I moved them onto a pillow covered with towels – puppies purge themselves twice as often as they eat. That didn't prevent my wife from putting them in bed with us. I was trying my best to avoid forming a bond with these puppies, but my wife seemed all in.

By then end of day three, both pups were holding down food and their diarrhea was less. Time to try larger food portions. They enjoyed the yard. They regularly pointed cardinals and blue jays, holding their point until the birds flew away. They also pointed squirrels on the ground or pillaging bird feeders. The pups lowered their heads and slowly stalked their would-be prey, then break into a run when the squirrel ran off. Each time I saw them point, I'd begin their field training, telling them to 'Whoa!" and stroking the back of their tails to raise them as high as they could. Not even six weeks old and their hunting instincts were so strong! I begged my wife to do the same when she witnessed a point in progress, but she would stay parked on her wicker chair and yell, "BANG!" to scare the prey, thus breaking the point. Infuriating woman!

By the end of the week, they were eating well and had plenty of exercise playing with a neighbor's Jack Russell and another neighbor's two Weimaraners. I felt they could be ready to return to Geert, then Chloë had a violent purging from both ends and was lethargic all day. Zoë had a similar incident. They seemed fine the next day. I phoned

Geert, telling him that they were eating special food and it seemed they put on weight. I also mentioned the violent purging event and recommended I keep them another week. I could also transition them from the special food to Blue Wilderness puppy food. Geert agreed.

The second week resulted with huge improvements for Zoë and Chloë. No more purges. Healthy stools. Great appetite and consuming a mixture of Baby Birddog Food and Blue Wilderness Puppy food. They went for rides in my truck or my wife's car. They slept with us in my bed. They learned to sit and lay down. Chloë was the first to learn something or take an interest in fetching toys. Once Zoë observed Chloë having fun and getting attention, she quickly imitated Chloë and mastered it. And there were toys. Each day, my wife would buy a new set of toys and with their teeth coming in, they would pull the stuffing out of a soft toy or tear a rope toy to shreds. Barely six weeks old and they were learning so much.

I trucked Zoë and Chloë back to Geert after the second week. These puppies were alive, a bit small for six week old German Shorthair Pointers but packing healthy pounds on their little bodies. I was sad but relieved when I put them in Geert's yard. I became very fond of them and if I had to let them go, it had to be at that moment. I explained that they needed one more week of Baby Birddog and Blue Wilderness puppy food mixture before going with only the Blue Wilderness. Geert seemed glad that the puppies were ok, but he confided to me that it would have been better for him financially if they passed away. He was hoping to make a profit from the sales of the puppies. If he was able to sell Zoë and Chloë, it would not cover the sire fee he paid. He also thought it would be next to impossible to sell them with undocked tails.

I offered Geert $500 for Zoë and Chloë. He gladly took the money, and I loaded the puppies into my truck.

Come on girls, we're going home.

Bosquito

One of the biggest challenges encountered by parents of young children is to get the kids to go to bed. Late night should be reserved for parents. They need that time to unwind from the kids. It allows for restful sleep.

My two step-children continually challenged my wife and I when it was their bedtime. There was always something. Can I finish watching this tv show? There is something making noises outside my bedroom window. I want the dog to sleep in my room tonight, not with her. I forgot to brush my teeth. Excuse after excuse.

One Friday night, the kids were procrastinating going to bed and they were being more annoying than typical six and four year olds can be in this situation. After they exhausted all their excuses, they finally went into their bedrooms. Then the whining started.

"Dad. There's a bosquito in my room," Ryan wailed. 'Bosquito' was their term for an insect my wife called a 'mosquito hawk' which is actually a crane fly. It looks like a giant mosquito that could suck a few ounces of blood from its victim, but they don't bite humans at all. Crane flies are harmless but that didn't matter to the kids. To them it's a killer and it was in the house.

Sarah started with her own complaints, "I'm afraid of the bosquito..."

"Leave the bosquito alone," I said. "It won't bother you."

"It's going to bite me," Ryan cried.

"I'm scared," Sarah stuttered.

The bosquito wailing went on for several minutes. It was funny at first as kids crying over valueless things can be, but they carried on too long and it turned into an annoying distraction. Both kids crept into the hallway to voice their continued complaints about the bosquito.

"That's it! I'm going to kill the bosquito," I announced. I shot out of my chair, grabbed a magazine, rolling it into a makeshift club as I stormed passed the kids. They ran to sofa next to their mom.

"Damn bosquito," I yelled when I entered Ryan's room. I saw the crane fly on the wall. I took a swing at it, but it flew away. The magazine made a loud WHACK against the wall. I heard both kids gasp from the living room. I smacked the walls with the rolled magazine, yelling "Damn bosquito...I'm going to kill you...stand up and fight bosquito..." Then my evil sense of humor kicked in.

"Oh! It's on me!" I yelled and continued to pound on the wall. I also made buzzing sounds to get them to think the bosquito was attacking me.

"Ow! Ow! *(more pounding on the wall)* BZZZ...BZZZ... It's biting me!"

I stepped part way out of Ryan's room, only my head, right arm and right leg in the hallway with a look of pain and fear on my face. I quickly glimpsed the kids on the sofa trembling and hiding under blankets. Their mom was doubled over, laughing.

"AH! AH! IT'S GOT ME!!"

I threw myself back into Ryan's room, slamming the door. I flopped around on the floor, making sounds of a struggle adding more screams and buzzing sounds. The kids were screaming in the living room, yelling "Daddy run away! Daddy!" The dog ran to Ryan's door and tried to open it. I heard my wife making a sound that was screaming, laughing and hyperventilating all at the same time.

I let out one more "Ahhhhhhhhhh!" as I quietly cracked open the door lying face down on the floor of Ryan's room with my arm in the hallway. The kids were so scared they couldn't cry, they just sat there whimpering. Sally, the dog, was perplexed. She struggled with the decision to come into the room to aid me or go to the sofa and be with the kids. I stayed motionless for a few minutes. I could hear my wife struggling to catch her breath.

"Maybe we should check Daddy," Sarah whispered to Ryan.

"What if he's dead?" Ryan replied.

The whispering got Sally's attention and she went to the sofa with the kids. I was a little puzzled that they failed to notice their mom sitting on the kitchen floor breathing into a paper bag. Clearly, she was worth saving over me. Both kids built up courage sliding off the sofa. Slowly they crept down the hallway toward me. I was still motionless with my face down in the floor. When they were within arm's reach of me, I made buzzing sounds. Both screamed. Their screams surprised Sally, who barked. All three ran behind the sofa. Once again, their mom burst out laughing, screaming and hyperventilating on the kitchen floor. I was using every ounce of self-control to not laugh or move.

Sally padded over to me. I could tell she was observing me and looking back at the kids. I felt the breeze caused by Sally's feathery tail gently blowing on my face. I heard both kids debate with crying whispers whether to check on me or get help. Sally's tail wagging must have helped them regain their courage. They crept back down the hall toward me.

"Is he dead?" Sarah asked.

"Dad, are you alive?" Ryan asked. I didn't respond.

"Try shaking him," Sarah told her brother.

He reached over then gasped, "the bosquito is on him!"

157

The crane fly must have been on my shoulder and moved, because I felt Sally nip at my shirt.

"Sally killed bosquito!" Ryan exclaimed. A small quake of laughter escaped from me. Sally started licking the back of my neck and face. I figured this was a good time to come back to life. I rolled over with a moan. Sally was happy, aggressively licking my face and wagging her tail so hard her butt was shaking.

"Sally rescued Daddy!" Sarah rejoiced. Both kids hugged Sally as she continued her relentless licking.

"What happened?" I asked as if I had been knocked out.

"The bosquito got you."

"Yeah, bosquito got you. And Sally saved you."

"See what happens when you try to kill a bosquito," I said, "if you leave them alone, they won't hurt you."

Both kids hugged me as I sat up. I saw a pair of legs on the floor around the corner from the kitchen.

"Let's go check on your mom."

Hopeless the Toxic HR Manager:
Four Tales of Destruction

One of the most dangerous organizations within any company is Human Resources. It is very perilous because there are venomous persons in the organization known as Human Resource Business Partners. The title "Human Resources Business Partners" is a misnomer. They do not represent Human Resources as a whole. Human Resources departments are usually made up of several administrative groups, such as Payroll, Benefits, Training, and Travel, but the Human Resource Business Partners belong to the "Employee Relations" group. Prior to the 1980s, Employee Relations was commonly known as the "Personnel Office." This was the group that dealt with employee-employer issues. Personnel Office representatives or Employee Relations reps or HR Business Partners, regardless of their title, are the most hated people in a company – deservedly so. Using the title HR Business Partner does a disservice to the other groups in Human Resources because the loathing associated with the HR Business Partner tends to bleed over to anyone or anything under the Human Resources umbrella.

HR Business Partners are the most arrogant and the most clueless persons in the company. They believe they are privy to things that no one else is allowed to know. They also believe they have authority over all employees. When asked what their purpose is, the answer depends on who asked the question. The answer they provide to an employee is "HR Business Partners protect the rights of the employee." The answer they provide their employer is "HR Business Partners protect the rights of the company." The truth is: HR Business partners always protect themselves and their power over all others. HR Business Partners cannot define their value to the company in terms of the product the company produces. Engineering, Supply Chain, Production, Assembly and Test organizations can point to specific items of the product, or to the product as a whole, and claim they contributed to it. Human Resources cannot do that. Human Resources may attempt to explain they have indirect claim to aspects of the product, but there are three or more degrees of separation of indirect support to the product.

In 1994, I changed jobs and moved across the country. I went from an aircraft manufacturer that employed over 100,000 people to a small sized aircraft manufacturer in Savanah, Georgia with less than 3000 employees. The Savannah company had a 'mom-and-pop' business feel about it despite building one of the most expensive private use airplanes in the industry. The Human Resources department had about a dozen employees, of which only two were in the Employee Relations group.

Less than seven years later, the company was purchased by a large Aerospace and Defense conglomerate. It became a wholly owned subsidiary within the conglomerate, but certain business operations from the new mother corporation were eventually injected into the smaller company. The concept of Human Resources Business Partners came from the home office, as did the flawed practice of embedding a HR Business Partner in every functional and matrixed organization within the company. Employee Relations rapidly grew into a bloated department. Rather than being facilitators, HR Business Partners assumed authority in areas that were not supported by corporate policy. Their assumed authority went unchecked by the executive leadership; and without means to reign them in, HR Business Partners became the cause of a very toxic and hostile workplace.

The most notorious HR Business Partner from that era was known as "Hopeless" by the employees of the company. Hopeless was responsible for causing irreversible damage to hundreds of careers during her tyranny. What is to follow are four tales of destruction attributed to Hopeless – the toxic HR Business Partner.

Part I: Cowboy

Wendy was a dispatcher in the Flight Test Maintenance department. Dispatchers typically ran parts from storerooms to the mechanics and technicians on the hangar floor or in the laboratories. Dispatchers also helped create parts kits and coordinate the use of ground support equipment. The Flight Test Maintenance department consisted of 50 employees that were predominantly male; however, there was one female mechanic and one female electrician in the department. Wendy, along with Terri, were two of the three dispatchers in the department. Physically, Terri and Wendy were opposites. Terri was tall – Wendy was short. Terri was medium to large build – Wendy was petite. Both ladies were as tough and ribald as their male coworkers, and they were respected for it.

The Flight Test Maintenance team enjoyed listening to the radio while working in the office and in the hangar. In the morning, all radios were tuned to the local radio station that played *Lex and Terry*, a nationally syndicated radio show based in Jacksonville, Florida. The team loved listening to *Lex and Terry*, and Wendy was no exception. If engine runs or other activities took them away from listening to *Lex and Terry*, those maintenance team members that had access to the radio were obligated to tell the others what happened on the show.

One of the electricians named Ron would call the show occasionally identifying himself as 'Ran,' a backwoods redneck that would get into trouble with his family and neighbors. Ran was not a fictional character. Ran was Ron's neighbor who was given the nickname Ran because he frequently 'ran' away from the trouble he caused. Ron didn't want to appear as a nosy tattling neighbor, so he would imitate Ran when talking about what Ran did.

One morning, Wendy was telling a small group of maintenance coworkers what she heard on *Lex and Terry* earlier that day. The show had a cast member named Brenda who was talking about the bad night she had. Brenda described how there was a terrible storm and her dog Cowboy got away from her. She was chasing after the dog, calling after him, getting very upset with the dog's lack cooperation as the storm got worse. Wendy told the group about how Terry, the radio host, was making fun of Brenda; and with enthusiastic play-acting, she imitated Terry imitating Brenda by sinking to her knees and crying out, "Please come Cowboy!"

What seemed to be a normal working day turned into turmoil when security guards escorted Wendy from the facility at lunchtime. The maintenance manager made inquiries about Wendy to Security only to be told that Human Resources notified them she was terminated and had to be taken out. It took a few days for the Director of Flight Test to get the reason for Wendy's termination.

During Wendy's animated replay of what was heard on the radio, Hopeless was in earshot and witnessed what she concluded was a description of a sexual act. Without conducting an investigation or making inquiries, Hopeless filed a report to herself that Wendy was initiating a sexual act while on her knees surrounded by male coworkers, asking them to "Please cum cowboys." Hopeless included in her report that termination was the recommended disciplinary action. The report and disciplinary action were immediately approved by her supervisor.

When the Maintenance team discovered the reason for Wendy's termination, several team members went to Employee Relations to explain about the radio bit, how Cowboy was a dog, the dog's owner was calling to her dog saying, "Please come Cowboy," and that Wendy was retelling the story to coworkers. They explained there was no sex

162

act involved. They told Hopeless that she misunderstood the entire situation. Wendy was an important member of the Maintenance team, and she should be rehired immediately.

"What's done is done," was Hopeless' reply, soon to be known as 'Hopeless Mantra Number One.'

The Maintenance team was infuriated. The Maintenance Manager spoke up to Hopeless, telling her that the Flight Test Maintenance offices and hangar is restricted to non-Flight Test personnel and that she had no business being in the area. Hopeless immediately cut him off, claiming he was about to perform an act of retaliation. She then chastised the Maintenance team saying that all those involved in Wendy's demonstration could face disciplinary actions for being associated with 'unbecoming behavior' in the workplace.

Hopeless finished the discussion with Mantra Number Two, "Let it be a lesson to you."

Part II: Mechanical Engineering

I was in a meeting called a Customer Advisory Board, or CAB, to provide support to my supervisor as he described features of a future aircraft the company was planning to manufacture. The conference room was filled owners and operators of legacy aircraft produced by the company. The CAB was a means to gain feedback directly from customers regarding desirable features and capabilities for future products.

The CAB took place in a small auditorium in the new design center. Rory's presentation was projected on the wall behind the podium. Microphones with push to talk switches were on the tables for attendees to provide comments or ask questions. Rory was wearing an earpiece that received a direct transmission from the microphones.

Rory was discussing the architecture of the new brake system for the landing gear of the new aircraft. Using a laser pointer, Rory drew attention to an animation that showed the articulation of the brakes. He explained the components of the system, describing two cylinders arranged in the classic "Master-Slave" configuration, among other parts. He was nearly done discussing the items on the slide when he paused a few times, looking as if he was going to say something off-topic. He was struggling to complete the description of the system and finally stopped.

"Hopeless, I will discuss your issues in private," he said addressing the group. He raised his hand to his ear. He moved his head back and forth a few times, then removed the earpiece and asked me to continue the presentation. He apologized to the attendees for having to step out, then introduced me to continue in his place.

I watched Rory walk to the back of the auditorium. Hopeless was waiting for him near the entrance. He pointed to the doors indicating to Hopeless that she needed to leave. He escorted Hopeless out of the auditorium and a conversation ensued in the hallway.

Hopeless took offense to the Master-Slave description in the presentation. It was clearly racist, in her opinion. She claimed she stopped the discussion before a customer took offense. Rory told her that the Master-Slave system was classic engineering terminology. He tried to explain how the Slave cylinder reacted to the output of the Master, but she refused to listen. They went back and forth about the terminology.

"Hopeless, everyone in that auditorium understands what a Master-Slave system is. It's been used in the Engineering lexicon for over a thousand years. They know it's not a racist term. You're the only one that thinks it could be racist."

Hopeless replied, "It takes only one person to be offended, then it has to be changed. It's in everyone's best interest."

Rory countered, "You're just trying to pick a fight. You don't understand the term or the principle of the system. You're going to insist on changing a thousand years of engineering because of your ignorance so you could feel good about yourself. That's not how it works Hopeless. What are you doing in this meeting? This is a Customer Advisory Board with a very select invitee list. You're not supposed to be here."

Hopeless lectured him that she was a Human Resource Business Partner and that she could come and go as she pleases. It was her job to observe all the employees as they worked, even in meetings. Rory told her that was a load of BS. She was probably there because there was an elaborate buffet lunch for the attendees. He told Hopeless that he was not changing the presentation and that she should leave because she was not cleared to be in the CAB. Hopeless informed Rory that she was filing an incident report, and she will need the presentation for her report.

Rory reminded Hopeless that he was a Senior Director in the Program Management Office, and he had the authority to deny her request. He also stated that she should not proceed with such a frivolous endeavor. She refused.

The case went all the way to the Legal Department, but as the case was elevated through the Executive Leadership Team, Hopeless increased the level of disciplinary action she wanted enforced on Rory from a written reprimand to a written condemnation with probation. A Senior Legal Counsel decided the whole 'incident' was not worth pursuing and dictated to the Human Resources department down to Hopeless that her incident report was filed in error.

By pursuing a case against Rory, Hopeless earned the dislike of several senior directors and two vice presidents. But little did they know that they were now on Hopeless' hit list.

Part III: Shue

When I became the Program Manager of an Advanced Technology Demonstration team, I inherited a group of engineers, mechanics, technicians, supply chain and administrative personnel. I also received a laboratory located across the airfield from the company's main facility. The Advanced Technology Laboratory was an old Quonset hut that was previously used as a maintenance hangar for small general aviation aircraft, like Cessnas and Pipers; however, it was large enough to squeeze two Gulfstream V-sized business jets inside.

One of the administrative personnel I inherited was a girl named Shue. She was a temporary employee, contracted with one of the office assistance companies such as Kelly or Manpower, although I do not remember which specific company she was from. Shue was of mixed Southeast Asian descent and a single mother in her mid-20's. I remember her as a gregarious person, which is good for some that worked as an administrative assistant and receptionist.

Shue wasn't the only mid-20's person in the Lab. Half of the engineers were recent college graduates that had been working less than two years with the company. One of the young engineers was a talented kid named Patrick, and Shue had a crush on him. Patrick was about five feet, seven inches tall, with dark hair and a slight build. He looked as if he was too young to shave. Patrick was shy around women; and authority figures (like me) made him nervous. For weeks, Shue sent Patrick signals that she was interested. Shue would always make an extra effort to greet Patrick each time he entered the offices from the parking lot or the hangar. She would offer to make him coffee or would bring him a sweet roll in the morning. Patrick was not interested. He had a girlfriend from college, who was still attending school in Virginia and was visiting him often. As the weeks went by, Shue began to dress more provocatively. Tight slacks or skirts. Her blouses became tighter and sheerer, and less buttoned. Patrick's coworkers teased him, as did I, about Shue flirtations. On more than one occasion, Patrick was told that he may have to man-up and take one for the team, to which he would roll his eyes and laugh it off.

We also had a young mechanic, named Rios, who was also in his mid-20s. He was a tall, thin Latin-African American. Rios was a contract employee with incredible skills. He was a bit quiet, but very friendly and self-motivated. I targeted Rios for direct employment. He was a great asset to the team. Shue liked Rios too. She didn't give Rios gifts, but her flirtations were obvious to all in the office. Rios slowly returned interest, and sure enough, he could be seen at Shue's desk leaning over to talk to her in whispers. Shue played as if she was attentive, but when Patrick walked by, she would shift in her seat to make sure Patrick could see her. Shue may have been trying to get a jealous reaction out of Patrick, but he was glad that she was flirting with someone other than him.

The Advanced Technology Laboratory was one of many labs within the company. The facility housed three fixed-based simulators adjacent to the major assembly building at the main plant. The administrative assistants supported all the labs. Sometimes Shue would spend part of the day at one of the other labs when they were short-handed of administrative assistants. It wasn't uncommon to see Torrie or Nikki from the other labs in the Quonset hut bringing supplies to Shue.

One day, Torrie entered my office in an agitated state, closing the door immediately behind her. She proceeded to tell me of a discussion she had with Shue earlier that day. She said Shue appeared upset and told Torrie that Rios was stalking her. He was calling her at home during the night. He would tell her that he wanted to come over for sex. Shue told Torrie that she was afraid for her safety and the safety of her daughter.

"What did you tell her to do?" I asked Torrie.

"I told her she should talk to HR," Torrie replied.

I thanked Torrie for telling me about the conversation. Shue was in the Quonset hut at her desk. I thought that if Shue spoke to HR about being harassed, I would have heard something by now. I decided the best thing to do was to tell Rios to avoid Shue until further notice. I called the shift manager, asked him to send Rios to my office and that Rios should use the back entrance.

When Rios arrived in my office, I told him that he was to stay out of the office area until further notice. I told him that I was told there might be an issue with him that involved Shue and he needs to avoid her until the matter was resolved. He said that she had been calling him after work for several days. Rios said that Shue was inviting him over, but he never went there. I told him that it was obvious to the entire staff that he and Shue flirted with each other, usually at her desk. He claimed that stopped a while ago. That was probably true, I thought to myself, I hadn't seen him at her desk in a while.

"Why did you give her your cell number?" I asked.

"I didn't," he replied, "She took it from the Emergency Contact List."

I repeated my orders to avoid Shue. I said that my information was second hand, and the purpose of my orders was to prevent any escalation of tensions between them. He asked if Shue made a report. I told him I didn't know. He asked if I would talk to Shue to request that she not contact him anymore. I said that I would.

Rios' statement about Shue using the Emergency Contact list to get his phone number for her personal use made me very concerned. I wondered who else she may have called. At that moment, I saw Patrick walking past my office door.

"Patrick! You got a minute?"

Patrick stopped in mid stride. He skulked into my office like a kid caught in the middle of making mischief.

"Has Shue ever called you after work hours?" I asked him.

"Oh yeah," he replied.

"Did you give her your number?"

"Nope."

"How'd she get it?"

"From the Emergency Contact list. She admitted to it."

"How often did she call you?"

"Every night for a while there. She hasn't called since I had my girlfriend answer the phone."

I decided to talk to Shue. I'd begin by asking about the Emergency Contact list and see if she would volunteer information about using it. I could then reprimand her for inappropriate use of a fellow employee's personal information. If she hadn't spoken to HR, then my reprimand would be at the head of the incident timeline and perhaps I could influence the outcome of future HR action. It seemed to be a good plan, but Shue left early that day. It would have to wait until tomorrow.

I walked through the hangar the following morning. Rios had been servicing a set of tires when I asked him how his day was going. He showed me the incoming call log on his cell phone. Shue's number filled the screen. She called him numerous times but didn't leave a message. I told him it was time to discuss his situation with Human Resources. He said he didn't want to cause any trouble and was apprehensive about discussing it with HR. We talked about it for a while, but I convinced him to have his shift lead arrange for a meeting with HR.

When I entered my office, Hopeless was sitting at the conference table.

"I need to use your office," she said smugly.

"What's going on?" I asked.

"There's been a sexual harassment incident. I need to talk to a mechanic, Rios. The lab maintenance manager is out sick today, so I'll need you to participate in his place."

Rios came to my office through the back entrance. He closed the door after entering. Hopeless introduced herself and the slaughter began.

"Rios," she began, "A report has been filed that you have made unwanted advances toward a fellow employee during working hours and that you have been stalking her outside the work area. That behavior is unacceptable. You are terminated. I will notify your contract house as soon as you are escorted off the premises. Your personal belongings will be shipped to you. Sign this."

She shoved a form across the table to him along with a pen.

"Hopeless, aren't you going to investigate this?" I asked. "Doesn't he get an opportunity to explain to you what has happened?"

"It really doesn't matter," she replied. "Sexual harassment is immediate termination."

"But there is no due process," I rebutted, "and it has been brought to my attention that Shue initiated this whole thing by abusing confidential information!"

"She called me!" Rios exclaimed, "She's been calling me nonstop for weeks. She wanted me to go to her house for a hook up and then she started demanding money and I didn't want to have anything to do with that psycho girl!"

"Shue has stated that you have been harassing her and that she has never contacted you," Hopeless countered and she invoked mantra number one, "what's done is done."

"Hopeless, I just learned yesterday that Shue has not only harassed Rios, but she has also been harassing at least one other engineer in this building. She used the Emergency Contact List to gather their home and personal cell numbers…"

Rios' cell phone began ringing.

"…and Rios is one of the best mechanics in the lab. You can't deny him due process…"

"She's calling me," Rios interrupted.

"What?" I asked. I glared at him, then at Hopeless. He showed me his phone. The number of the incoming call was Shue's desk phone.

"Answer it," I told him, "on speaker."

"Hello?"

Shue's voice came over the speaker, "Hey Rios, can we have lunch today? We can go to my place…"

I motioned for him to go on mute. He did.

"I'm going to call her desk. We should hear the incoming ring on his phone," I said. I dialed Shue's desk number and sure enough, the ring could be heard coming from Rios' phone. I then took his phone and motioned that they follow me. We walked over to Shue's desk where she was still talking – not knowing there was an audience listening. The phones echoed when we got to her desk. She was caught and completely oblivious as to what just happened.

"Well Hopeless," I said, "the harassment charge that was filed was a lie. Revoke the termination."

"The termination has already been approved. What's done is done."

I argued with Hopeless for another 30 minutes. I asked Hopeless to show me the company policy for investigating harassment claims. I wanted her to show me where in the policy she was allowed to issue a termination without conducting a proper investigation.

"You're not entitled to see it," she said firmly. "You need to drop this crusade to keep Rios. He's a contractor. We don't need an excuse to fire him."

"Are you going to terminate Shue?" I asked.

"No, that would be retaliation," Hopeless said.

"But she's only a contractor," I countered.

"If she believes she was fired over filing a sexual harassment claim, then we are exposed legally," she said.

"So, the first one to file a harassment claim is always the winner," I concluded, "Is that how it's going to be? Is that the precedent you want to set?"

Hopeless wouldn't budge. She took Rios' badge and walked him out of the building. I had the shift lead gather Rios' personal items. The mechanics and engineers met Rios at Bailey's Cockpit after work to give him his items and say their goodbyes.

I sent Shue to the labs at the main facility for the remainder of the day. I asked one of the Finance Department managers to send me an email that should notify me that I had an immediate budget cut, and I was to reduce headcount. I forwarded the email to the Human Resources Contractor Support group, bypassing Hopeless, giving them permission to contact Shue's contractor house that her services were no longer needed.

Part IV: Darnell

As a Program Director, I was managing sixteen suppliers that provided the Flight Controls systems and components for a new airplane that my company was developing. Some were legacy supplier companies, a few were new to contracting with my company; and three suppliers were international. At times, I was stretched thin trying to maintain oversight to all of them simultaneously. One supplier in particular was very difficult. It was based in Southern California. The supplier provided the actuation and control electronics for the primary flight control system. It could not maintain schedule. It could not deliver any analysis, reports or models on-time. The only time it seemed to make progress was when I would spend a week at their facility. During one visit, I encountered an old friend that worked for a military aircraft manufacturer who was also visiting the troubled supplier. He had similar issues and kept a small team of engineers on-site. He told me the supplier didn't have enough people to work all the contracts it had; the same group of engineers supported five other aircraft projects, including mine. It was clear that I needed a full-time presence at the supplier.

I hired a Program Manager, named Darnell. He had a strong background in mechanical systems and very good project management skills. I informed the supplier that it was getting 'help' in the form of Darnell. The supplier was not happy. The supplier's Program Managers repeatedly said that Darnell was not needed and that they thought his presence could be demoralizing to their engineers.

I told the supplier's management that they had plenty of opportunity to get on track. I tried to spin it that after my program manager has been on-site for a while and they get back on track, I may send him to oversee a different supplier in the area. They were not convinced. I had a feeling that Darnell could be entering a hostile work environment.

Darnell had been on-site for five months and I arrived with a team of engineers for a quarterly program management review, or PMR. During a break in the meeting, the supplier's Human Resources Manager approached me about an issue with Darnell. We retreated to her office.

"I received a complaint about your on-site rep, Darnell. Our laboratory manager, Damien, said that Darnell used inappropriate language and made threats to him in a meeting. There were several witnesses. Damien feels that Darnell purposely inflicted damage to his reputation."

"Have you talked to any of the witnesses about the allegation," I asked.

"I received the compliant a few days ago and I've just started the investigation. I wanted to let you know about it."

"Thanks. I'm surprised I haven't heard anything about this from any of the engineers."

"I'll let you know the results when I have concluded the investigation. I will also need to contact my counterpart at your company. Who should I contact?"

I gave her the phone and email information of the assistant HR Business partner, Amanda. I didn't want Hopeless involved. Amanda was the only person in Employee Relations that I believed was worth having around. I had dinner with Darnell that night and informed him about the complaint.

"I didn't use inappropriate language or make any threats,' Darnell told me. "I told Damien that he hadn't shown progress since I've been here and that if it's reported to you that all hell will break loose."

"I know about Damien," I said, "He was lazy and always had an excuse for his poor performance on the previous program. I don't know why they assigned him to this program."

I told Darnell to keep the conversation confidential so he would not compromise the supplier's HR investigation. He said he would continue as if he knew nothing about it. The remainder of the PMR was the usual bad news I came to expect from the supplier. When I returned to Savannah, I contacted Amanda to confirm our Employee Relations department received the complaint about Darnell. Amanda confirmed she had a conversation with the supplier's rep, but Darnell's case was reassigned to Hopeless. Days later, Hopeless barged into my office with a Level Three disciplinary action for Darnell.

The Disciplinary Actions had four levels. Level One was a verbal reprimand to the employee with a written record entered into the employee's HR file. Level Two was a written reprimand with a corrective action. If the corrective action was not completed to the satisfaction of the supervisor, then a six month probation was enforced. A Level Three action was a written condemnation with corrective actions, training and an eighteen month probation. If within the eighteen months of probation, a complaint of any kind is made against the employee, then the action is elevated to Level Four and the employee is immediately terminated.

Hopeless handed me a form to sign. In the "Reason for Disciplinary Action" box it read **Employee acted inappropriately using abusive language and threatened physical violence**. That was it. Nothing else.

"Where is the summary report of the supplier's HR investigation?" I queried Hopeless.

"It's not needed. It was reported to me by their HR representative. That's all I need to go forward with a disciplinary action," she replied.

"No way Hopeless. There is a process that needs to be followed before judgement is made, and yours is not the sole opinion. I have a say in this as well. He's my employee."

"And you're lucky you don't have a disciplinary action against you as well. You're his boss and you're responsible for his behavior."

"Don't threaten me," I told her. "I want to know what happened. I know the guy that made the complaint. He was a poor performer on the previous program that involved that supplier. When this project was kicked off, I told the supplier they need to put someone else in charge of their lab because that guy was no good. He's acting the same way he did before. When he doesn't perform, he creates a diversion. How do you know this isn't all BS?"

"It doesn't matter. The complaint is against Darnell, not the other way around."

I told her I wasn't going to sign it. We got our supervisors involved in the conversation: the director of Employee Relations, Hopeless' boss, and the Vice President of the program, my boss. Hopeless and her boss argued that they considered it a valid complaint because they were notified by a follow HR person and that since Darnell was an employee for less than a year, technically he should be terminated. I argued that they should not be reacting to hearsay and we should have all the facts before a decision toward a disciplinary action is considered. They countered that it was already filed in their system and if Darnell was such a good employee, it would be easy for him to breeze through the probation period. My boss caved in. He told me to sign the form.

I brought Darnell to Savannah for three weeks. I initially told him to plan for three weeks of training that was required for a new employee, but I told him the truth his first day in town. I prepped him for the meeting with Hopeless when he was going to get the disciplinary action. He was very upset. He had relocated from North Carolina to Southern California for this job, and now he thought he was targeted for failure. I said we had a chance to expunge it from his record when the supplier's HR report was issued, and it proved the accusations were false.

Darnell sat through Hopeless' belittling session, holding in all his frustration and anger like a real trooper. I bristled when he signed the form accepting the disciplinary action. Either he signed it and we moved on; or he would get fired. I was determined to get his employee file cleared as soon as possible. I used the time he was in Savannah to introduce him to everyone on the program, attend training classes, and prepped him to begin working with other suppliers if his current assignment got any worse.

Darnell was sent back to the supplier after his three week exile was completed. Two months later, it was time for another quarterly PMR. I was back at the supplier's Southern California facility for the meeting. During the months between the PMRs, I did not receive a status regarding the investigation into the accusations against Darnell. At the end of the first day of meetings, I went to the supplier's Human Resources Managers office. I inquired about the investigation. The HR manager informed me the investigation was completed shortly after she notified me of the compliant. During her investigation, Damien admitted to embellishing the entire encounter. There was no abusive language and there was no threat of physical violence. Damien was frustrated and he believed the conversation would have led to abusive language, etc., and he felt that he needed to report it. I asked if she had notified my company's Employee Relations representative about Damien's admission. She said she had discussed the matter with Hopeless. I told her all about the disciplinary action Darrel received and that I wanted to get the whole matter erased from his record. She agreed to help. I asked her to contact the Vice President of Human Resources at my company and to please keep me up to date with the conversations.

When I returned to home base, I confronted Hopeless about the matter. She tried to spin it a positive way that by receiving the disciplinary action, Darnell was on his way to becoming a better employee through all the training and diversity classes he took. I fired back that there should not be a bad mark on his employee record for an accusation that never happened, but all I received from her were mantras one and two: what's done is done, and let it be a lesson to him.

I went above Hopeless to her director, but I received the same response. I did not understand why they would not correct a huge mistake such as this from an employee's record. I decided that I had one final chance to fix it. In the program Vice President's weekly staff meeting, I told the Vice President about the conversation I had with the supplier's Human Resources manager and that the entire episode was a lie. I also asked him that I needed his help to convince Hopeless that Darnell's record should be cleansed. The other Directors in the meeting were unaware of the complaint. When I mentioned it in the meeting, they immediately voiced their support to clear Darnell's record. Hopeless turned red in the meeting. I thought I had her in a corner, but she played a trump card. She leapt to her feet and with her left hand on her hip and pointing a finger at me she said, "Don't you tell me how to do my job! Just because I'm a woman doesn't give you the right to threaten me this way!"

I was now on Hopeless' list of enemies. Darnell was terminated before his probationary period was over. He was told it was because the supplier's performance did not change, but no one in his chain of command approved the action.

Montreal

As a Program Manager for a major Aerospace corporation, I had to travel regularly to supplier locations for quarterly Program Management Reviews, or PMRs. The PMRs usually took two full days filled with meetings. Many times, the supplier hosted a dinner/social gathering after the review. Ironically, the amount of money spent on the dinner was relative to the amount of bad news that was discussed during the PMR.

One supplier, Thales, was based in Montreal, Canada. In May of 2012, I travelled with a fellow program manager, John, and five engineers to Montreal for the second quarter PMR. The company I worked for was in Savannah, Georgia. Nearly all our travel was on Delta Airlines. At the time, Delta had a flight from Atlanta to Montreal on a regional jet. For me, regional jets are not good. At nearly seven feet tall, a regional jet is a very cramped, uncomfortable experience for me. For six hours, I was crammed into a small seat with no leg room. Getting up to stretch and move around was not an option. If you can't stand up straight in the aisle of the airplane, you won't be able to stretch properly.

We stayed at the Marriott hotel in Montreal-Trudeau International Airport. Sure enough, our gate was at the opposite end of the airport when we arrived. One of the two rental cars was reserved in my name, so I had to get it before checking into my room. John received a message from the Thales customer representative that they wanted to take us to dinner tonight. The message provided a location and time to meet. By the time I checked in to my room, I had only 15 minutes to change clothes for dinner.

A full-sized car in today's nomenclature is complete bullshit. A 1970 Buick Electra is a full sized car, not the 2012 Nissan Sentra provided by Hertz. A Sentra doesn't even qualify as a sub-compact car – it's a goddam roller skate. We gathered in the hotel lobby to divide up into the two vehicles for the drive to dinner. I gave my car keys to Serge. I still felt cramped and achy from the RJ. He was only five and a half feet tall. He could do the driving tonight.

We were met by the supplier's two program managers (Marc-Anton and Franz), Chief Engineer (Thalia) and Contract Manager (Trish). The restaurant had outdoor dining with several long tables under a large canopy. It was a beautiful evening, mild weather for late May in Montreal. We were enjoying wine and pleasant conversation when a group of women walked through the dining area banging on pots, pans and pot lids with wooden spoons. They marched around the tables and around the perimeter of the canopy. One woman came up to me banging her pot lid with a large smile on her face trying to encourage me to clap along with her clatter. Most of the diners joined in, then the pot-ladies left, taking their ruckus with them to the next place.

I was thinking, what the hell was that? Some weird Quebec tradition? Our hosts explained that it was called 'casserole'. Even in Quebec, its Italian name was also used: cacerolazo. Coincident to our visit, student tuition fees were hiked by the government. The casserole was a form of protest by the mothers of the students, to take casserole

179

pans and make a large noise in the streets. Oh well, I thought, better than gunfire.

The next morning, we all met in the lobby to discuss our agenda prior to the meeting with the supplier. We were about to leave when two familiar gentlemen approached John and me. They were Van and Bart, two vice presidents of Parker, another supplier from Irvine, California. It was obvious they were here to meet with Bombardier – the major aerospace manufacturer in Montreal. We exchanged greetings. They asked to meet for dinner. We had a PMR scheduled with their company in two weeks. They wanted to discuss the upcoming PMR and their status. We agreed to meet them in the restaurant bar by 6PM.

Our meetings with Thales dragged on all day. I started experiencing leg pain midway through the day. By mid-afternoon, my right leg was noticeably swollen and warm to the touch. I broke out in a complete sweat. During one of the breaks a Thales engineer, Claudia mentioned a walking trail in the business park. She was pregnant and walked to perform her daily exercise during our break. I agreed and we all went walking with her. I had suspected my leg pain was due to a blood clot. I had deep vein thrombosis, DVT, before but that was years ago in 1989. I had no clotting issues since. But once you've had a DVT, you know what the pain is. Taking the walking break confirmed to me that I developed a DVT. It probably started on the flight to Montreal and all the sitting I had been doing the past two days aided the development of the clot. The pain was now getting worse as I put weight on the leg. I was perplexed about developing the DVT because I was taking a drug called Pradaxa at the time. I was taking Pradaxa because of an atrial fibrillation condition I had in 2010. Pradaxa is a blood thinner to prevent blood clots in the heart and lungs. Back in 2012, it was not approved for DVT, but I couldn't understand why it wasn't preventing a DVT after taking it for over a year.

During the remainder of the meetings, I formulated a few plans in my mind as to how I could get out of the dinner meeting with the Parker VPs. I decided I'd meet them in the bar for a drink, then excuse myself for not feeling well. I needed to inform John that he would have to participate in the dinner meeting by himself. As we drove back to the hotel, John mentioned that I didn't look so good. I told him I was feeling under the weather and that I would see if I could get my blood pressure checked when we got back to the hotel. He asked if I would be at dinner, and I replied that I would meet everyone for a cocktail but probably not stay after that.

When we arrived at the hotel, we agreed to meet in the bar five minutes before 6PM. I went to the concierge desk and asked if the hotel had a nurse on call or a nurse station nearby. After all, the hotel was attached to the largest airport in Canada, so there had to be a paramedical station somewhere in the airport.

"Sir, do you need an ambulance?" the concierge asked in English with heavy Quebec accent.

"No," I replied, "I would just like to check my blood pressure, I think it's elevated."

"Sir, we can transport you to hospital?"

"No thank you. That is not what I need."

"You do not feel well?"

"Just a little off," I said as I turned toward the elevator.

"May I call someone for you, sir," the concierge asked.

"No, that's not necessary," I said, trying not to show my annoyance.

I cleaned up as best I could in my room. I looked terrible. I was covered in sweat. My hair clung to my head. I took off my pants. My leg was swollen and warm to the touch. Portions of the calf were red – not quite a rash.

I returned to the lobby to meet John. I avoided eye contact with the concierge when I walked toward the bar.

"How are you feeling?" John asked.

"I'm feeling off. I'll stay for a cocktail then excuse myself. Does that work for you?" I asked John.

"Sure. No problem," John replied.

The Bijou Resto bar was immediately adjacent to the hotel lobby. The differentiating feature between the lobby and the bar was the maître d' podium signifying the entrance. High boy tables and chairs were laid out between the podium and the bar, which was located next to a large panoramic window providing a view of the airfield.

John and I sat at a table beside the window. We ordered our beverages and discussed the results of the day. The waitress set the drinks onto the table, then her attention was diverted toward the entrance of the bar. A man with a racing bicycle was talking to the hotel concierge and maître d'. He was wearing spandex biking shorts and shirt, a helmet, fanny pack and a Day-Glo yellow vest with the word E M E R G E N C I E blazoned across the front and back. John and I sat up a little straighter to see what was happening. All three were looking at us. The concierge pointed at me and the man with the bicycle began to weave his way through the maze of tables with his bicycle towards me.

Oh shit, I thought to myself. What the fuck is to going to happen now?

"Excusez-moi, avez-vous une urgence médicale?" inquired bicycle man. I was dumb with astonishment, I couldn't reply.

"Parlez angleais, s'il vous plait," John replied in French for me.

"Je ne parle pas anglais," he answered. He doesn't speak English and I don't speak French– this was getting worse, I thought.

"No emergency," I said shaking my head and making hand motions.

"No?" he asked.

"I asked about blood pressure," I said pantomiming a cuff on my bicep. "It was a misunderstanding."

He was trying to understand. He took off his fanny pack and rummaged through it. I shouldn't have tried to explain to him. The bar was filled to quarter capacity and every patron was watching our exchange. He emptied the contents of his pack onto our table, looking at me with an inquisitive glance. It was first aide items: bandages, gauze, hydrogen peroxide, hand sanitizer and iodine. At this point, I was hoping for narcotics. Not only was I embarrassed and frustrated, all the stress was giving me a bad headache.

"Pas d'urgence," John said, "Malentendu."

"Ah," he said nodding his head. He packed the first aide items into his fanny pack. He weaved his way back with his bicycle to the maître d'. I explained to John how I asked the concierge for a nurse to check my blood pressure and how I thought the whole issue was resolved until just now. The bicycle man talked with the maître d' and concierge for a few minutes, then pedaled away into the airport.

The Parker executives arrived. The bar area had filled with customers nearly to capacity. We ordered another round of beverages. While we discussed business, our waitress brought menus so we could order dinner from the bar, then be seated in the dining room when the food was ready. We continued our conversation and perused the menus for a few minutes. The waitress returned to take our orders and I sensed that it was time to make my excuse about not feeling well and retreat to my room.

She was about to take our orders when Bart said, "What's going on there?"

At the entrance were two paramedics with a gurney, the concierge and the maître d'. The concierge and maître d' pointed to our table and sure enough, the paramedics began weaving their way with the gurney through the bar toward us. Oh shit, not again, I thought. John was about to say something, but I shot him a mean glare.

"You have emergency," a paramedic said in broken English with a heavy Quebec accent. "Get on!"

"No emergency!" I said. At that point I decided it was best to get out and try to resolve the situation away from the growing crowd. I walked out of the bar with the paramedic team and their gurney snaking their way through the maze. Everyone was watching and I was using every ounce of self-control.

I strode to the concierge and asked, "Is there a room where I can talk with you and the paramedics in private?"

The concierge opened a door behind the front desk. A paramedic shoved me into the room, pushing me onto a chair. His partner started unloading medical containers from the top of the gurney onto a table. When the last box was unloaded, the paramedic slammed the door shut.

"You are having heart attack?" he asked.

"No," I replied, "My blood pressure is elevated. What are you doing?"

He grabbed a blood pressure cuff from one of the containers and wrapped it on my arm. He then reached to my shirt and literally ripped it open, popping every button off the shirt. He saw my chest hair and muttered something in French. *At this point in the story, I should explain that the hair on my chest and abdomen is long. Very long. I joke about it being long enough to braid.* The paramedic produced a razor out of nowhere and proceeded to shave the hair off my chest with fast and deliberate upstrokes sending hair flying everywhere. His partner set up an electrocardiogram machine, plugging it into the wall, connecting cables, etc., the whole time the two of them conversing in French. When the shaving was done, the second paramedic pressed electrodes all over my chest.

"Lean back, sit still," one said while pumping the cuff. I laid back quietly while they did the test. I just wanted to get it over.

"Your heartbeat is normal. Blood pressure elevated." Well no shit, I thought.

"Sir, why did you think you needed medical help," he asked.

I should have kept my mouth shut. With the way the whole day had progressed, I should have said I don't know, but I wasn't thinking properly at the time, and I let it slip, "I think I have a blood clot in my leg."

Both paramedics tore at my pants. Before I knew it my pants and underwear were down around my ankles. Both were squeezing the swollen areas of my leg muttering in French.

"Yes, we would agree that you may have a clot. We shall take you to hospital."

No way. I wasn't going to let that happen. I knew that if I was admitted into a hospital in Canada, and Quebec of all places, I wouldn't be released until someone from the U.S. came to Canada to collect me.

"Thanks, but no," I told the paramedics, "I'm sorry you were brought here. It was all a misunderstanding."

"But sir, you are in a medical emergency. You must be admitted to a hospital," he said.

"Nope. I decline,"

"You cannot decline."

"The hell I can't."

"By law, we must take to hospital. You have been declared a medical emergency."

"Undeclare me. I'm not going to hospital. I have declined your diagnosis."

I didn't understand Canadian medical law. A patient cannot decline treatment according to their socialized medicine. Me being a foreigner on a business trip made it more complicated because I'm the responsibility of the Canadian government. I found out later that the paramedics could be held liable if I died after refusing treatment.

"No. You must come with us," the paramedic said.

Then I went for the nuclear option with a shitload of American attitude.

"The only one getting on that gurney is the two of you if you don't leave me alone," I told them in a threatening voice. There I was trying to project an aura of intimidation with a ripped shirt and my pants down around my ankles.

"This is most unfortunate. You must sign papers."

The second paramedic opened a container and withdrew a six inch wide binder filled with legal documents.

"You must sign each page. I must read to you. Then you read back to me. Then we sign," he said. And he proceeded to read each page, first in French, then in English, then I had to repeat the page to him in English, then I signed and dated the bottom of the page, and the two paramedics placed their initials beside my signature. After 30 pages, I lost count.

"It is less paperwork if you would let us take you to hospital," the paramedic stated after each page was completed.

When the final page in the binder was being processed, the second paramedic packed up the medical equipment into their respective containers.

"We hope you do not die before to go home," the paramedic told me. They opened the door to the lobby, piled their containers on the gurney and walked away. There I was on a chair naked with a ripped shirt and pants around my ankles and in the doorway looking in at me was the concierge, John, my other coworkers and the two Parker vice presidents.

"What happened?" one of the guys asked.

I adjusted my clothes as best I could and walked out of the room to the concierge station.

"Got any aspirin?" I asked the concierge. He opened a drawer and handed me a half-full bottle of aspirin. I took it, turned toward the elevator.

"I'm retiring for the evening. I may see you in the morning," I said to the crowd.

Epilogue

Needless to say, it was a restless evening. I was physically and mentally spent with the ordeals of the day. I took three aspirin and double the amount of Pradaxa I normally take for the evening. I was in a lot of pain. I remember lying in bed thinking I may not survive the night. The next morning, I repeated the double Pradaxa and three aspirin dosage and decided to take three aspirin every four hours during the return trip to Savannah. My logic was to change a DVT issue to a bleeding issue, which seemed a bit more controllable at the time. When we got to Savannah, I informed my coworkers about the suspected DVT. They offered to take me to Memorial hospital, but I told them I needed to go home and arrange care for my dogs before I am admitted to a hospital.

It turns out I did have deep vein clots in my leg. I was admitted for three days.

www.ingramcontent.com/pod-product-compliance
Lightning Source LLC
Chambersburg PA
CBHW051422090426
42737CB00014B/2788